BS 580 .J53 S84 1971
Stevenson, Herbert F.
Three prophetic voices:
studies in Joel, Amos and

DI

Puritan Reformed Theological Seminary
2965 Leonard Street NE
Grand Rapids, MI 49525
USA
616-977-0599

THREE PROPHETIC VOICES

By the same author:

A GALAXY OF SAINTS
JAMES SPEAKS FOR TODAY
THE ROAD TO THE CROSS
TITLES OF THE TRIUNE GOD

THREE PROPHETIC VOICES

Studies in Joel, Amos and Hosea

HERBERT F. STEVENSON

Editor: Life of Faith

Foreword by

REV. PAUL S. REES D.D., LITT.D.

FLEMING H. REVELL COMPANY
OLD TAPPAN, NEW JERSEY

MARSHALL, MORGAN & SCOTT LTD.
BLUNDELL HOUSE
GOODWOOD ROAD
LONDON, S.E. 14

© H. F. Stevenson 1971

All rights reserved. No part of this publication may be reproduced, stored in a retrieval system, or transmitted, in any form or by any means, electronic, mechanical, photocopying, recording or otherwise, without the prior permission of the Copyright owner.

ISBN 0 8007 0515 7

Printed in the United States of America

Foreword

Although scholars have lately taken a fresh interest in it, most of us in the circles of the pious have not of late exposed ourselves to the fire-power of the Old Testament. This, I think, is notably true of the twelve prophets that are clustered at the end of its thirty-nine books. The only thing "minor" about them is their relative size—less in quantity than an Isaiah or a Jeremiah.

Herbert Stevenson has taken three of the twelve and, like battleships that have been "mothballed," has reactivated them. Their big guns are allowed to hurl their well-aimed shells again. Joel warns. Amos denounces. Hosea pleads.

The Holy Spirit has preserved these potent documents as vivid, virile tracts for the times. They have in them predictive elements that look forward and these, because Hebrew thought is less sharply concerned with relationships between past, present and future than that of Western man, are not always easy to disentangle.

What is far more immediate in impact is the powerful commentary on the social and religious conditions that surround the prophets and those whom they address. The call is for action—facing up to the mischief of idolatry, the shame of injustice, the hollowness of religious ritual divorced from practical obedience, and the certainty of judgment unless there be a right-about-face.

All this Mr. Stevenson helps us to see and feel.

He has dug in. He has pondered. He has weighed and measured his words. He has suggested applications to contemporary situations—sometimes leaving us wishing he had gone beyond mere suggestion to direct, spelled-out relevancies.

And I for one feel that by what he has produced he has put us in his debt. For, as Dr. G. Campbell Morgan once put it, "There is no question that these Hebrew prophets have a voice for our times."

PAUL S. REES

Minneapolis, Minnesota

Contents

Introduction

The Minor Prophets are a neglected section of Scripture today: their stern note, addressed to an apostate people, falls harshly upon the ears of a spiritually complacent generation. But it was never more needed than now, for conditions prevailing in the Western world, even in the church, are strikingly similar to those in Israel when these prophets spoke forth the word of the Lord. Especially is this true of Hosea, Joel and Amos (though they did not prophesy in that order, and in considering their books we rearrange them in chronological sequence).

For a right understanding of these books, however, it is highly desirable to study them in the *Revised Standard Version*, as well as in the Authorised. Many passages which are obscure in the *AV* become crystal clear in *RSV*. In some passages, however, the newer rendering has unwarrantably altered the meaning; and so both texts are used in this exposition: basically the *AV* is followed, except where *RSV* is preferable. It will be manifest in every instance which is being quoted. Excerpts from the *RSV* are used by permission.

This book is not a commentary but an expository, devotional and practical study of these three Minor Prophets, which stand first in the Canon; they are intimately related, and constitute a trilogy. Critical problems have been carefully considered and taken into account, but are not discussed since they are fully treated in the standard commentaries—to which I acknowledge indebtedness, and particularly to H. L. Ellison's *Men Spake From God* and *The Prophets of Israel* and J. K. Howard's *Among the Prophets*. Originally published as articles in *Life of Faith*, these studies have been revised and in some cases rewritten.

The manuscript of this book was in the hands of the printer when the *New English Bible* rendering of the old Testament was published, and so no use could be made of it. Also, the *New Bible Commentary Revised* (IVF) appeared at that time, so allusions to the *IVF Commentary* refer to the edition of 1953, and not the virtually new "revision," in which the prophecies of Hosea, Joel and Amos have all been entrusted to new contributors, who sometimes adopt different viewpoints and interpretations from those expressed in the original volume, and quoted here.

I would once again express heartfelt gratitude to Dr. Paul Rees, whose encouragement stimulated the publication of my first book, *Titles of the Triune God*, fifteen years ago. His Foreword to that volume was invaluable in introducing a new author, especially to readers in America; and his continuing friendship has been expressed in Forewords to three succeeding books, which have greatly enhanced them all. Now for a fifth time Dr. Rees lays me deeply under debt, by a Foreword for which all readers of this book will be keenly appreciative, as I am. Also I would warmly thank Prof. F. F. Bruce for his encouragement, and for reading the manuscript and making invaluable suggestions incorporated in the book.

A Prophetic Trilogy

Some parts of Scripture are strangely neglected, even by many who vigorously affirm that the Bible is the Word of God from cover to cover. But since "all Scripture is given by inspiration of God, and is profitable . . ." then inevitably such neglect must mean spiritual loss. This is particularly true of the so-called Minor Prophets, which generally are given only scanty attention, except for a few arresting verses (usually taken out of context), the story of Jonah, parts of Daniel and the graphic imagery of Haggai.

Perhaps the chief reason for this neglect is that their message is, for the most part, sombre. They lived in days of apostasy, and had to give stern warning—albeit with tender entreaty and impassioned appeal for repentance and return to the Lord—that continuance in evil ways would bring inevitable and terrible judgment. These solemn tones in the prophetic ministry are not popular today, any more than when they were first given: but they come insistently, in days alarmingly comparable to those in which the "minor" prophets lived and spoke. (Incidentally "minor prophets" is an unfortunate misnomer, given solely for the reason that their books are not so lengthy as those of the "major prophets." Some of them are equally forceful, pertinent and valuable as any OT literature.)

Three of these books are particularly arresting and relevant—the first three of the twelve, as they appear in our Bibles. The lives of Joel, Amos and Hosea overlapped (in that order), assuming the early date of Joel; they thus form a trilogy of prophetic utterance to a generation hastening toward "the day of the Lord." They were the first of the "writing prophets," though which of them was the pioneer in that respect is vigorously debated by the critics, each of the three being supported by certain scholars. It is not our present purpose to enter into these disputations: we accept the substantial evidence for the conservative opinion, that Joel prophesied in Judah during the minority of Joash (2 Kings 12 : 1ff), about 830 BC, and so was the first of the three. Amos also was a Judaean, but prophesied in Israel, about 760 BC, bringing to the northern kingdom a stinging condemnation of its apostasy, and pronouncement of impending judgment. Hosea spoke God's final word to Israel, in the quarter-century before its destruction, 750–725 BC. Their lives were thus overlapping; their ministries complementary and cumulative.

Their day and generation bore a remarkable resemblance to our own. The people of Israel—southern and northern kingdom alike—instinctively religious, had yet turned their backs upon God, and worshipped the twin deities of materialism and sensuality. Israel especially, although maintaining nominal allegiance to Jehovah, had degraded the "worship" at their sanctuaries to virtual idolatry, including sexual licentiousness. To both kingdoms, a succession of prophets brought the Lord's rebuke, appeal and warning. Judgment upon such apostasy was inevitable. Joel saw it afar off, for Judah: but the southern kingdom was as yet not nearly so apostate as Israel. The prophets to the northern kingdom, however, had a more immediately urgent message. Israel—or Ephraim, as Amos repeatedly called it—was judged first, for two reasons. Not only was its departure from God more absolute, its cup of iniquity full, but also by its separation from Judah and the house of David it had disavowed true allegiance to God and the royal line of His anointing. Judah, less depraved at this period in its history, was destined to be the vehicle of the fulfilment of the prophecies to the patriarchs and the divine promises to David.

The book of Hosea was given pride of place among the Minor Prophets in the Hebrew Bible, not for chronological reasons, but because of its greater length than others; and also for its winsome, appealing character. Amos unquestionably prophesied some years earlier.

The patience and persistence of God, in His grace toward sinful men, are demonstrated as well as declared by the prophets. His longsuffering is an essential aspect of His character. But alongside this revelation of truth is the complementary fact that a term is set to the exercise of divine forbearance. Scripture consistently links together the compassion of God with His righteous judgments. The Old Testament has much to say about the "day of the Lord," and the New Testament about His Second Advent—both signifying an end to the "day of grace" and the breaking forth of judgment. The longsuffering of God to Israel was manifest in the ministries of many prophets, over many generations. Hosea was the last of God's messengers to the northern kingdom, and his book uniquely blends the winsome note of the Old Testament "Gospel" with the final pronouncement of long-delayed doom.

Time and again these prophets might be speaking to our generation equally as to their own. Study of their books is therefore by no means academic: here is a vital word of the Lord for today. These prophecies survey the contemporary scene from the divine standpoint: they also indicate the task of the messenger of God in such a situation. Penetrating yet compassionate diagnosis of the spiritual malady, clear warning of its consequences, and impassioned appeal for repentance and return to the Lord: these are the authentic prophetic notes. Moreover, these books teach us the necessity of persistence in preaching the word of the Lord, even though it seems to fall on deaf ears, so long as the day of grace endures. There will come a time when mercy gives place to judgment: and in view of it, we should witness with compulsive urgency.

I

JOEL

PROPHET OF PENTECOST

JOEL: PROPHET TO JUDAH

No one knows for certain who Joel was, or when he lived. His name, which means "Jehovah is God," was a common one among the Jews in all periods of their history. The fact that he describes himself as "the son of Pethuel" (1 : 1) is equally unrevealing, for Pethuel is otherwise unnamed in Scripture. One thing alone is indisputable: he lived in Judah, and prophesied to that southern kingdom. His book indicates that he did so at a time of national declension from godliness. Alas, there were many such times; the problem posed by this book is, just when did Joel utter his warnings and admonitions?

There are two schools of thought among Bible students, on this question. Some conservative scholars strongly affirm an early date, before the rise of Assyria to power. Among those favouring it are the *IVF* and *Wycliffe* Commentaries, and H. L. Ellison. Many others, including the majority of modern scholars, favour a late date, after the Babylonian exile. The choice lies between these two extremes; internal evidence rules out any other period of Judah's history.

It is not our purpose to discuss the pros and cons of this critical debate; we accept the arguments in favour of the early date, which places Joel's ministry during the minority of Joash, and while Jehoiada was regent. If this is correct, Joel was the first of the "writing prophets," and a senior contemporary of Amos and Hosea, prophets to the northern kingdom. Therefore, although the dating of the book is not of vital importance, as we shall see, the early alternative has much to commend it.

I

"This is That . . ."

JERUSALEM was agog with excitement. Its streets were thronged with Jews from every part of the known world, gathered in the holy city for the feast of Pentecost. But it was not merely anticipation of the temple ceremonies, and of the social enjoyments of the occasion, that accounted for their extraordinary commotion. There was some intangible, ecstatic element in the air which made their pulses race and sensibilities tingle.

Strange rumours had run like wild-fire through the crowd in that incredible fashion which defies analysis or description; rumours associated with the group of fanatics who persisted in believing in Jesus, the self-proclaimed Messiah from Galilee, whose pretensions had been rejected with scorn by Israel's religious leaders and who had been ignominiously crucified by the Romans. Yet these fanatics had the effrontery to assert that this Nazarene, despite the utter refutation of His claims implicit in His death, was indeed the Christ; moreover, that by that very death upon the cross He had made atonement for sin; that He had risen from the dead, and by His triumph over the tomb had proved Himself to be the Son of God and Saviour of Israel.

Further, these zealots now declared that, ascended to the throne of the Majesty on high, He had, in fulfilment of one of the astounding predictions He had made, sent His Spirit—the Spirit of God—to be with and in His people for ever. There were wild stories of phenomena attesting this claim: that the house where these fanatics had been huddled together, had been shaken as by a rushing mighty wind; yet it had not collapsed or even been damaged. More amazing still, tongues of fire from heaven had appeared, and lighted upon every one of the group; yet they had not been stricken by lightning or suffered harm. On the contrary, they were there present before them all, rejoicing and praising God. That something strange, miraculous, had happened to them was unquestionable: these people who had cringed in fear of the consequences of avowing themselves disciples of Jesus, were now openly proclaiming themselves as such; and in a manner which astonished the hearers. They *looked* different: their faces were radiant; they manifestly were utterly convinced that what they said about this Jesus was true. They *spoke* differently: no longer diffident, they affirmed with intense conviction that Jesus was alive, was the true Messiah and Redeemer of Israel.

Even more astonishing was the fact that, as these uneducated Galileans spoke, the "Jews of the dispersion" who had come from so many different parts of the world, heard what they said *in their own languages and dialects*! It was inexplicable: nothing less than a miracle. Of course, as always, there were clever folk ready with a glib answer to every situation, who scoffed at the idea that this was miraculous; and the "funny ones" who tried to turn it aside with a jest: "These men are full of new wine!" It's nothing but a drunken orgy!

At this point one of the fanatics stood up—he was readily recognised by many in the crowd as Peter, a fisherman of Galilee who had been one of the most intimate associates of this Jesus—and began to speak. As he did so, a strange silence fell upon the turbulent crowd; for this rough fisherman spoke with a tone of authority, with a fluency of language, indeed, with a prophetic unction—had they but known it, Spirit-given—that commanded a hearing. "Ye men of Judaea, and all that dwell at Jerusalem," he said, "be this known unto you, and hearken to my words: for these are not drunken, as ye suppose, seeing it is but the third hour of the day. But *this is that which was spoken by the prophet Joel . . .*"

Now Peter's words give us an authoritative guide to the understanding and interpretation of the prophecy of Joel. His declaration had, in fact, a two-fold effect: it indicated that Joel's prophecy explained the phenomena of Pentecost; and that Pentecost provided a key to the prophecy. But just as Pentecost does not stand alone in God's dealings with men—it is one of a sequence of events in the fulfilling of the divine purposes—so Joel's prophecy of Pentecost does not encompass and explain all that his book contains.

Pentecost was a landmark in the on-going purposes of God determined from eternal ages, and finds its place in relation to the Incarnation of the Son of God at Bethlehem, His earthly life and ministry, His atoning death, resurrection triumph, ascension to the throne on high, the enduement of His disciples with the Holy Spirit as His redeemed people and the instrument of the calling out of His church from among all nations—unto the glorious consummation at His appearing and reign as King of kings and Lord of lords. So also the prophecy of Pentecost in Joel is central to his message: there is much before it, and much follows. Inevitably, what precedes it has to do with man's sinfulness and failure; with divine judgment and mercy—judgment inevitable, because God is God; and yet mercy prevailing over judgment, because God is the God He is—the God and Father revealed ultimately in our Lord Jesus Christ: a God of compassion, ready to redeem His wayward people even at infinite cost. Equally inevitably the prophet looks beyond the travail, for both God and man, occasioned by human guilt, to the ultimate triumph of God over evil; of mercy and truth prevailing over guilt and judgment; of the will of God being done in earth as it is in heaven. He foresees the subduing of all adversaries of God and His people; calm after the storm of earth's final, fiercest battle—that Armageddon which may be nearer at hand than many of us care to believe.

2

Jehovah's Commentator on Current Events

JOEL is quite unlike any other of the Old Testament prophets. He does not stand forth and declare, "Thus saith the Lord . . ." —although the opening sentence of his book claims the prophetic office for him in the familiar terms, "The word of the Lord that came to Joel . . ." But his manner of making known that word is quite distinctive from that of other prophets. Indeed, in the beginning of his prophecy he appears more like a commentator upon current events than a prophet of God. He might be regarded as an Old Testament counterpart of those television experts who explain to the uninitiated just what the present happenings involve and imply. In similar manner Joel says to his contemporaries, "Do you really understand what is happening? There is much more to this plague of locusts than you imagine, you know."

But there is this vast difference in Joel's admonition from that of the modern commentator on current affairs: he explained what was happening as the spokesman of the Lord. He made no speculations or guesses, but declared authoritatively the real nature of Israel's plight, and what it portended. His prophetic ministry was exercised in a different manner from that of other prophets, but it was equally "the word of the Lord," apposite to his day and prescient concerning the future.

Joel is an enigmatic prophet. Unlike Hosea, of whose family life we are told so much, Joel is absolutely unknown to us except by his name—which means, "Jehovah is God"—and the fact that he was "the son of Pethuel" (1 : 1). Joel was a common name in Israel; and the prophet cannot be identified with any of the several other Joels mentioned in the Old Testament. We do not even know for certain when he lived: the pundits are divided in opinion between an early date, or centuries later, after the exile. We here are unconcerned with these critical arguments, though personally convinced of the early date. Whichever period is correct, the message of the book is unaffected. As Calvin observes, "As there is no certainty, it is better to leave the time in which he taught undecided; and, as we shall see, this is of no great importance." The earlier date, however, makes Joel a contemporary of both Hosea and Amos, those prophets to the northern kingdom to whom his book is so akin.

Whoever he was, Joel was a literary genius. Hebrew scholars tell us that his book is the most perfect example of polished poetry and prose in the Old Testament Canon. His vivid imagery fires the imagination, even of English readers: the description of the invasion of locusts in chapter one is so graphic that it makes the reader almost cringe before their all-consuming assault.

Plagues of locusts were no uncommon experience in Israel; and tragically devastating they were. Yet *this* invasion was unprecedented. It is generally agreed that the various terms used—palmerworm, locust, cankerworm, caterpillar—refer either to different varieties of locusts or to stages in their development. Israel had experienced previous disasters on their account; but Joel, Jehovah's commentator upon the present predicament, asks, "Has anything like *this* ever happened before? You aged men, can you remember such an invasion as this, of wave upon wave of locusts? Doesn't it imply something especially significant; can't you see the Hand of God in it?" One is reminded of the words of a greater than Joel, who, years later, said to *His* generation, "You know how to interpret the appearance of the sky, but you cannot interpret the signs of the times" (Matt. 16 : 3).

In a scornful aside to reprobates, Joel says, "Awake, ye drunkards, and weep; and howl, all ye drinkers of wine . . . for it is cut off from your mouth" (1 : 5). His prophecy as a whole, however, is remarkable for the fact that he says so little about the sin of the people which occasioned the divine judgment. He does not denounce them, in the manner of most of the prophets, nor expatiate upon the divine wrath called forth by their sin. That the plague of locusts and the accompanying drought *were* a consequence of national sin, he just takes for granted; and he gives warning that this is but a precursor of yet sterner judgment if they should not repent—"Alas for the day!" he declares, "for the day of the Lord is at hand, and as a destruction from the Almighty shall it come . . ." (1 : 15).

What, however, should Judah do in the meantime? Joel told them. "Be ye ashamed, O ye husbandmen; howl, O ye vinedressers, for the wheat and for the barley; because the harvest of the field is perished" (1 : 11). Those who suffered most through the failure of their harvests, had a responsibility for that failure. They might have been good husbandmen and vinedressers; and they might have blamed the whole tragedy of the situation upon factors outside their control—upon the drought, the locusts, even upon God. The clear implication of Joel's indictment, however, is that *they* bore a full share of responsibility for their plight. Not lack of rain, nor the plague of locusts, but the sin of the nation was the real cause of their condition. And the sin of the nation was the sin of individuals—of the husbandmen and vinedressers, as much as anybody else. They were, as we are, so apt to throw the blame upon the community, rather than face up to their own share of it; perhaps they even condemned, as we do, their "permissive age," their sinful generation. But such generalised sentiments were not enough: God is concerned with individuals, one by one: with you and with me. "Be *ye* ashamed. . . ."

Joel, addressing others in this personal way, did not exclude himself. As he entered into the distress, not only of his people but of the very beasts of the field (1 : 20), he turned to the Lord in agonised petition: "O Lord, to thee will I cry . . ." (1 : 19). Only when we become personally involved, in prayer as in prophecy, can we speak with convicting power to the conscience of our day and generation.

An arresting feature of chapter 1 is how Joel indicates the travail of nature through the calamitous consequences of man's sin. It is a distressing fact, hinted at rather than fully set forth in Scripture, that "the whole creation has been groaning together until now," because "the creation was subjected to futility, not of its own will but by the will of him who subjected it in hope . . ." The "hope" of creation, as of redeemed mankind, is "the revealing of the sons of God . . . because the creation itself will be set free from its bondage and decay, and obtain the glorious liberty of the children of God" (Rom. 8 : 19–22).

In addition to this condition of "futility," or "vanity" (*AV*), nature shares in the effects of specific judgments upon mankind. "The field is wasted," Joel says, "the land mourneth . . . the vine is dried up, and the fig tree languisheth" (1 : 10, 12). And again, "the seed is rotten under their clods, the garners are laid desolate . . . for the corn is withered" (1 : 17). But he speaks especially poignantly of the suffering beasts—suffering through no fault of their own, but for man's selfishness and sin. "How do the beasts groan! the herds of cattle are perplexed, because they have no pasture; yea, the flocks of sheep are made desolate" (1 : 18). While there is no warrant in Scripture for the excessive adulation of animals so frequently indulged today, they are repeatedly mentioned as objects of God's creation and concern; and as such, to be treated with consideration and compassion. "The beasts of the field cry unto thee . . ." (1 : 20); and by implication, He hears their cry.

The main burden of Joel's message, however, lies in the *robbing of God* which human sin and its consequences entail. The very judgments of God despoil *His* land: "For a nation is come up upon *my* land . . . he hath laid *my* vine waste, and barked *my* fig tree (1 : 6–7). It is a reminder that the land was not theirs, but God's; they held it in trust for Him. But they had regarded it as their own; they had thought only of their prosperity and pleasure, and neglected His claims upon them. One is reminded of our Lord's parable of the vineyard entrusted to husbandmen who refused to render to their master his rightful due, but sought instead to possess entirely for themselves what he had entrusted to them.

There is a very pertinent application to our own day of this abiding principle of the divine governance, of the world in general and of the church in particular. We are apt to regard both as if they were ours, existing for our benefit and subject to our will; whereas in fact we are accountable to their rightful Lord, for our conduct in both spheres. What of *our* stewardship, as a nation, and as a church? Are we rendering to the Master the fruits He has a right to expect?

Joel stresses this aspect of the calamities of his day, again and again. "The meat-offering and the drink-offering is cut off from the house of the Lord" (v. 9. cf. vv. 13, 16). There is a two-fold implication in these dramatic words. By the cessation of the appointed offerings, God was deprived of the worship of His people which they represented and expressed. Unhappily, what should have been truly a delight to Him and a means of grace to them, had become merely a religious ceremony. The sacrifices and offerings, instead of expressing their repentance for sin, their adoration and worship, their submission and thanksgiving, had gradually degenerated into valueless repetitive acts of ritual. God had been robbed of their true worth before He sent the judgment which caused those sacrifices to cease.

Here another aspect of the situation should have smitten their conscience and aroused their concern. The ceasing of the sacrifices *deprived them of the appointed way of approach to God.* They had depleted the offerings of their spiritual value; so God had taken those offerings away from them. He would not allow the holy ceremonies of the sanctuary to continue as perfunctory ritual, carried out merely as a matter of tradition and habit.

Once more Joel speaks to our own day as insistently as to his own. We all know that failure to cherish intimate relationship with God, through prayer and the reading of His Word, and neglect of the means of grace, result in a deterioration of spiritual life and service, until these become barren and burdensome. Then, when some calamity or vicissitude of life drives us again to seek the face and help of God, we discover to our consternation that the "way of access" to the throne of grace which we so foolishly neglected, seems closed to us. Only *seems*, we hasten to add; while life lasts there *is* an open way for the truly penitent and utterly sincere. But it needs to be stressed that the entail of sin and backsliding is serious; forgiveness and restoration do not always speedily follow upon a realisation of our plight. There is a New Testament counterpart of the "meat-offering and drink-offering cut off from the house of the Lord."

What should we do in such a situation? Joel addressed his appeal to the priests—those who, most highly privileged, had sinned most seriously in relation to the sacrifices and offerings. First, he called upon them truly to repent: "Lament like a virgin girded with sackcloth for the bridegroom of her youth . . ." (1 : 8). As a bride rendered desolate by the loss of her bridegroom just before her marriage, they should mourn *their* desolation in the loss of their vocation and station at the altar of the Lord. "Gird yourselves and lament, ye priests," he urged; "howl, ye ministers of the altar: come, lie all night in sackcloth, ye ministers of my God: for the meat-offering and the drink-offering is withholden from the house of your God" (1 : 13).

But it is not enough to face the fact of past failure; nor even to repent. "Sanctify a fast," Joel exclaims; "call a solemn assembly . . . and cry unto the Lord" (1 : 14). The time for action had come! There *was* something they could do about the plight they were in. In a situation where nothing else would be of any avail, they could cry unto the Lord: and therein lay their only hope.

If ever there was need for earnest waiting upon God, that He might grant revival from on high, it is today. God is robbed of the worship and praise that are His due; and the people are languishing for the bread and water of life. The only hope for our generation lies in the remnant of the Lord's people, who wait upon Him day and night for the opening of the heavens in reviving grace. The summons to us, as to Israel in Joel's day, is "Cry unto the Lord . . ."

This is the more urgent and solemn because present distresses are but foreshadowings of that "day of the Lord" which might be nearer than a somnolent church seems to think. The term "day of the Lord" occurs frequently in the Old Testament, always signifying divine judgment—sometimes in a limited sense, in visitations of chastisement upon a wayward people, such as the plague of locusts; but always with allusion to that great and terrible day of final judgment. That day might be for us, as Joel declared, "at hand"; and moreover, "as a day of destruction from the Almighty shall it come."

From the Almighty! That name for God expresses, not so much His omnipotence, His irresistible power, as our rendering conveys; but rather, His munificent grace. *El Shaddai* is perhaps the most tender, most moving of all the divine names and titles. It tells of Him as the Fount of all good, and Sustainer and Comforter of His people. When such a God—a God of compassion and bounty; the God and Father of our Lord Jesus Christ—sends destruction, who then shall be secure? Thanks be to God, all who truly know Him as *El Shaddai*, our Heavenly Father, in Christ Jesus our Redeemer and Lord.

3

Sound an Alarm!

HAVING delivered his inspired comments upon the disaster confronting his fellow countrymen through the "invasion" of hordes of locusts (ch. 1), Joel proceeds, in chapter 2, to warn them that this catastrophe is but the forerunner of a much more terrible judgment if they should fail to learn its lessons and repent of their sins. The devastation caused by the locusts might take on the dimensions of a calamity of the first magnitude. Instead of abating, the plague might strip them bare and reduce them to utter destitution. The prophet therefore calls upon the priests and "ministers of the altar"—already summoned to "sanctify a fast" and "call a solemn assembly" (1 : 14)—to "blow the trumpet in Zion," and "sound an alarm in my holy mountain" (2 : 1). This was a situation as serious as war, and the nation should act accordingly. The awesome "day of the Lord," Joel declares, is "nigh at hand."

There has been much discussion among Bible students regarding Joel's use of this term. The "day of the Lord," spoken of by many prophets, always refers to a specific and terrible divine judgment upon an unrepentant people. It found partial fulfilment, later, in such calamities as the conquest and scattering of Israel, the northern kingdom, by Assyria; and the subjugation and captivity of Judah by Babylon; and this plague of locusts, the prophet gave warning, might well become a major crisis in the history of the nation. In all prophecies concerning the day of the Lord, however, the final judgment is ultimately in view. Often it is difficult to discern between the limited and more immediate fulfilment of certain oracles, and their ultimate realisation when Christ shall come to reign. That is so here in Joel 2; the warning of the potential consequences of this plague of locusts merges with the vision of the great "day of the Lord" which is still future.

In vivid and dramatic language, the prophet likens these all-pervading locusts to invading armies, irresistible in their onslaught. They are comparable to the chariots and horses of conquering raiders; the devastation which marks their progress is like the "scorched earth" left in the wake of marauders who wreak havoc with fire and sword (2 : 5). Indeed, some commentators think that Joel sees in the locusts a foreshadowing of attack by alien armies —they are symbolic "heralds," as it were, of the Assyrians; but the majority of Bible students agree that the passage throughout has the locusts alone in immediate view. The most startling aspect of their advance, however, lies in the fact that the locusts are accomplishing the purposes of God: He is in command; this judgment is of Him (2 : 11).

The language which Joel uses in this passage, and also later in his book, is termed by the scholars "apocalyptic," because it describes visions granted to the "seer" relating not only to events happening at the time of utterance, but also to the future. It is said that apocalyptic writing was developed and flourished in the post-exilic period; and for this reason, primarily, Joel is regarded as one of the latest of the prophets. Indeed, so conservative a writer as Stephen Winward, in his book, *A Guide to the Prophets*, declares that Joel "belongs to the period of passing from prophecy to apocalyptic," and that the book is "prophecy on the way to becoming apocalyptic." As if the inspiring Spirit were limited in His giving of the Word to literary fashions! Another reason for relegating Joel to a late date is that he allegedly quotes from several other of the prophetic books. But it might equally well be that Joel was one of the earliest, and that others quoted from him!

Be that as it may, all interpreters are agreed that this vision of Joel was made known to the people of his day as a preparation for a most moving call to repentance. Until the hour of judgment arrives, all the prophets declare, there is a way of escape from it through heeding the divine admonition. The call to "rend your hearts, and not your garments, and turn unto the Lord your God: for He is gracious and merciful, and slow to anger . . ." (2 : 13) has been made familiar to most of us by the librettist of Mendelssohn's *Elijah*, who with poetic licence puts these words of Joel into the mouth of that still earlier prophet. Some of us can never read this stirring appeal without associating it with the melting music of the oratorio.

This is indeed one of the most moving of prophetic utterances: Joel piles adjective upon adjective to extol the readiness of God to respond to repentance on the part of His people. He is gracious—that is, "*inclined* to pardon the repentant sinner" (Wycliffe Bible *Commentary*); merciful—the equivalent of "full of compassion"; slow to anger, and abounding in loving-kindness. What pardoning grace is envisaged here; what a tender Deity is described! The parody of truth presented by those who speak and write about the "savage God of the Old Testament" is exposed by this and countless similar declarations. But Joel adds a characteristic note: he says, "Who knoweth if He will return and repent, and leave a blessing behind Him; even a meat-offering and a drink-offering unto the Lord your God?" (2 : 14).

What a method of evangelism is this! Its emphasis is placed, not so much on personal blessing as a result of turning to the Lord, but on the restored means of grace: the refurnished altar, where God is worshipped as well as His people forgiven and renewed. Joel was jealous for the glory of God: that He should receive His due from His people, as well as they receive pardon and grace from Him. And how reverently reticent the prophet is—not committing the Lord to an automatic reaction to anything they might do, but rather throwing out the hint, "Who knoweth . . ." These words enshrine a promise, based upon sure knowledge of the divine character and principle of action, but expressed with consciousness of unworthiness to receive it, and reliance upon God's mercy and faithfulness alone.

Of course, personal blessing to a repentant people is implicit in Joel's evocative words, for the provision of a meat-offering and drink-offering envisages a restoration of the land to normality and the provision of a good harvest: but the overpassing of this aspect is significant of Joel's whole attitude to the situation, and his sense of values—the temporal being totally subservient to the spiritual.

Such a happy outcome is not yet assured, however; so Joel once again issues the challenge, "Blow the trumpet in Zion . . ." (2 : 15), but this time he uses, not the word for a war-alarm, but a summons to a solemn assembly, convened in the hope of divine mercy. He calls the people and priests alike to earnest waiting upon God, even with weeping and urgent prayer (2 : 16–17). If only they will heed, "then will the Lord be jealous for His land, and pity His people." In the Name of the Lord, Joel promises corn and wine and oil, those basic necessities of life in Israel in those days (2 : 19).

As his message from the Lord proceeds, Joel grows more eloquent still in telling of the divine bounty which will ensue from their repentance. Even the beasts of the field are reassured, and the abundance resulting from the "latter rain" is promised. Yea, the Lord will "restore the years which the locust hath eaten . . ." (2 : 25): a promise claimed by the people of God in all generations, turning to Him after spiritual drought and dearth due to acknowledged and abandoned waywardness. To the truly repentant the promise has ever come: "Ye shall . . . be satisfied, and praise the Name of the Lord your God, that hath dealt wondrously with you."

The last word in this section, however, is not concerned with the blessing of His repentant and restored people, wondrous as that truly is, but with the vindicated honour of His holy Name: "And ye shall know that I am in the midst of Israel, and that I am the Lord your God and none else: and my people shall never be put to shame" (2 : 27).

4

Pentecostal Outpouring

THAT the section foretelling the outpouring of the Spirit on all flesh (2 : 28–32) is central to Joel's prophecy, is emphasised by the fact that it comprises a separate chapter (ch. 3) in the Hebrew Bible. This also accentuates the distinction between this event and the promised temporal blessings attendant upon the repentance of Judah in Joel's day (2 : 18–27). Turning to God, and unfeigned trust in Him, ever evoke divine blessing; but Joel foretells that "afterward" shall ensue this greater, spiritual benefit. We have inspired interpretation of the passage in Peter's sermon on the day of Pentecost (Acts 2 : 16–21). He changes "afterward" into "in the last days"—a recognised term for this Gospel era, between Christ's coming in lowliness to accomplish His earthly ministry, and His Second Advent. Joel's prophecy, Peter explicitly declares, was fulfilled in the Pentecostal outpouring of the Spirit.

Undoubtedly both Joel and Peter thought that the "all flesh" to receive this gift, refers to all Israel: it took a vision from the Lord to convince the apostle that the Gentiles are included within the promise (Acts 10 : 9–16). When that fact was established, doubt arose within the church as to the range of the prediction: does it mean that ultimately all mankind will be endowed with the Spirit, or should the promise be limited to a certain number—those who respond to the grace of God made known in the Gospel—from among all the peoples of the earth? While universalists hold to the former view, the New Testament leaves no doubt in the minds of the majority of Bible students that Joel anticipates the calling of the church out from all nations. Here is a foreview of the Gospel going forth to the uttermost parts of the earth, and accomplishing the purposes of God in gathering unto Himself a redeemed people representative of the entire human race.

We have here, then, clear indication of the divine intention to indwell by the Spirit every member of His new-covenant church. From His earliest dealings with man, God had endued certain people with His Spirit, for specific commissions and responsibilities.

We read of the Spirit coming upon national leaders, endowing them with supernatural wisdom and strength for their appointed tasks; and certain gifts of the Spirit enhancing the skills of craftsmen in the making of the Tabernacle. Inspired utterance by the Spirit was given to prophets and psalmists. All these, however, were exceptional people, granted exceptional enduement by God for the fulfilling of tasks He entrusted to them.

The distinctive characteristic of the "last days," however—this dispensation of the church—is the coming of the Spirit of God upon, and remaining with, *all* His people, irrespective of race, sex, age or social rank. Now this, announced by a Hebrew prophet, is astounding. The Jews despised all Gentiles, regarding them as beyond the bounds of God's covenant calling and grace: if any desired to embrace the Jewish faith, they were reluctantly admitted as proselytes on suffrance, and not regarded as truly "within the fold." They had scant respect for women, and treated them as mere onlookers and not participants in the worship of the temple or synagogue. They venerated age, and kept youth "in its place." They held rigid notions of the "divine rights" of rank.

All this cherished pattern of life is swept aside in one sentence by Joel. Of course, he is not the only prophet, nor the first, to recognise that God's purposes reach out in grace to all mankind: that fact is clear in all the Scriptures, from the *protevangelium* pronounced in Eden. But Israel as a whole resisted the revelation, and clung ever more tenaciously to their conception of themselves as the covenant and only people of God. In this spirit, they applied to Israel exclusively the promise here made to "all flesh"; but Paul shatters this misconception in Romans 10 : 12–13, where he states categorically that "There is no difference between the Jew and the Greek (Gentile): for the same Lord over all is rich unto all that call upon Him. For"—and here is the verse which clinches the linking of the apostle's argument with this passage, since he quotes Joel 2 : 32—"whosoever shall call upon the name of the Lord shall be saved."

Not only should the Spirit be poured out upon all flesh, but "your sons and your daughters shall prophesy." In this dispensation of the Spirit, prophecy has changed its character from that of the ministry of the Old Testament prophets: Joel is not declaring that young fellows and girls should proclaim the oracles of God, "Thus saith the Lord . . ." and foretell things to come. That kind of prophecy reached its culmination and received its *congé* in John the Baptist. Prophecy in this Gospel age takes the form of carrying the good news far and wide; making Jesus known as Saviour and Lord. There is no limitation of this proclamation of the Evangel to any accredited "ministry"; it is the privilege of all believers to show forth, by word and deed, that "Jesus saves" those who come unto God by Him.

This is not to set aside, or disparage in any way, the office and functions of the ordained ministry: there is ample New Testament warrant for such, as recognised and exercised in the Reformed churches; but a priestly caste, claiming for itself mediatorial functions, and exclusive privileges in conducting the worship and witness of the people of God—as in the Roman church—is ruled out by this prophetic pronouncement. Here is refutation beforehand of Rome's entire hierarchical structure. Part of of Biblical heritage is the glorious doctrine of the priesthood of all believers—and the responsibility of all to "give a reason for the faith that is in them."

Most striking is the fact that "daughters" are given equal status and opportunity with "sons" in this prophetic witness; for although Deborah and other women were among the earlier prophets, the attitude of the nation toward women in public life hardened as time went on, until they were almost entirely excluded. The few who defied this tendency, such as Jezebel and Athaliah, seemed to confirm the wisdom of it. But in the church of Jesus Christ there is "neither male nor female," says the apostle Paul; though most churches exclude women from their ministries. We shall not linger on this controversial theme, however; it is enough to reassert that God made known His purpose, through the prophet—and reiterated it on the day of Pentecost—to equip women and girls, as well as men, by His Spirit, for the functions of New Testament prophecy. Calvin declares: "The prophet speaks not here of the public office of teaching, for he calls those prophets who were not called to teach, but who were endued with so much of the light of truth, that they might be compared with the prophets; and certainly the knowledge which flourished in the primitive church was such, that the meanest were in many respects equal to the ancient prophets."

Moreover, age distinctions also are obliterated in the exercise of the gifts of the Spirit. "Your old men shall dream dreams, and your young men shall see visions." Now dreams and visions were means—probably the principal means—by which the will and word of God were made known in those days. "As it was the usual way among the ancients," says Calvin, "that God manifested Himself by dreams and visions to the prophets, so he says 'your old men shall dream dreams, and your young men shall see visions': but the prophet no doubt sets forth under these forms of speech that light of knowledge in which the new church excelled after Christ appeared; he indeed compares the light of faith to prophecy . . ."

In Christ, the Self-revelation of God is complete. "God, who . . . spake in time past unto the fathers by the prophets, hath in these last days spoken unto us in His Son." (Note again the phrase "in these last days.") Maybe there was literal fulfilment of the prophecy concerning dreams and visions in the earliest era of the Christian church, before the Canon of Holy Scripture was completed; though we do not read in the New Testament of any inspired dream after Pentecost, and the only visions mentioned are those of Saul of Tarsus, on his way to Damascus—if that personal appearance to him of the exalted Lord can be described as a vision (Acts 9 : 1–9); of Ananias, concerning Saul's conversion (Acts 9 : 10); of Cornelius, that a man named Simon would visit him, and tell him what he ought to do (Acts 10 : 1–6); of Peter, on the housetop, concerning the conversion of Cornelius (Acts 10 : 17–19; 11 : 5); of Paul, hearing the call of the man of Macedonia (Acts 16 : 9), and later, in Corinth (Acts 18 : 9), and possibly on the ship during the storm on the journey to Rome (Acts 27 : 23); and finally, of the apostle John on the isle of Patmos (Rev. 9 : 17). When, however, the inspired Word of God was completed, with the writing of the books which constitute the New Testament, His people needed no further revelation of His mind and provision and will. We hear occasionally of dreams or visions which are said to impart special commission or spiritual enlightenment to the recipient; but while we do not deny the possibility of God meeting some particular need in this way in certain circumstances or situations, as a general rule we do well to be very reticent concerning such claims, for God has given in the Scriptures His full and final communication. As He illumines it by His Spirit, the Bible becomes to all His people their chart and compass, guide, counsellor and inspiration, in all events and experiences of life.

What, then, means this foretelling of old men dreaming and young men seeing visions? Whatever literal fulfilment it might have had during the apostolic era, it surely implies for us today that all the redeemed have equal opportunity of knowing and obeying the word and will of God. Not only do all have access to the Scriptures of truth, but all have the indwelling Spirit to make the Word "come alive"; to illumine and apply it to their personal needs, and for the accomplishing of their responsibilities as believers. Of course, in a metaphorical sense it is true that Spirit-quickened men of all age-groups "dream dreams" and see visions: did not Carey and Wilberforce and Martin Luther King, to name but a few amid myriad others; and do not the spiritual eyes of many aged saints remain undimmed, like the physical eyes of Moses at 120? For the promise was not only "unto you"—those who heard Peter speak on the day of Pentecost—but also "to your children" through all generations of this Gospel age, and "to all that are afar off, even as many as the Lord our God shall call" (Acts 2 : 39).

The final barrier to blessing broken down by the outpouring of the Spirit of God, was that of rank: for "also upon the servants and upon the handmaids in those days will I pour out of my Spirit." Now servants, in the days when the Spirit was given, were for the most part slaves; and as such they were regarded as possessions rather than persons—mere chattels. Joel foretells that this cruel distinction between master and servant would be disregarded by the enduing Spirit: He would treat both alike as temples for His indwelling. An effect of this is seen graphically in the new relationship brought about between Philemon, the master, and his runaway slave Onesimus, who upon his conversion became "a brother beloved" (Philemon 16). Truly in Christ not only there is "neither Jew nor Greek (Gentile)" but also "neither bond nor free"; yea, "there is neither male nor female: for we are all one in Christ Jesus" (Gal 3 : 28).

Commentators differ widely in opinion concerning the forecast of "wonders in the heavens and in the earth, blood, and fire, and pillars of smoke. The sun shall be turned into darkness, and the moon into blood, before the great and terrible day of the Lord come" (2 : 31). Many consider that these signs still await fulfilment immediately before our Lord's return. Indeed, the *Wycliffe Bible Commentary* says concerning this whole section, that Joel "dips into the future and sees spiritual revival in Israel and deliverance from all surrounding enemies. His vision thus anticipates a first fulfilment on the day of Pentecost and a final realisation in the complete victory of the kingdom of the Lord Christ." Accordingly, the phenomena described will occur at the end of the age, when the full outpouring of the Spirit will be upon repentant and restored Israel, and the "wonders in the heavens and upon earth" will be "wonderful portents of the approach of the judgment."

Others point out that Peter quoted the whole passage from Joel (2 : 28–32, cf Acts 2 : 16–21), and inferred that it related in entirety to the events then happening. Thus the IVF *New Bible Commentary* asserts that "Peter did most certainly identify the whole passage 2 : 28–32 with the day of Pentecost," and Professor F. F. Bruce, in his *New London Commentary* on *Acts,* suggests that "The wonders and signs to be revealed in the world of nature may have more relevance in the present context than is sometimes realised: it was little more than seven weeks since the people in Jerusalem had indeed seen the sun turned into darkness, during the early afternoon of the day of our Lord's crucifixion. And on the same afternoon the paschal full moon may well have appeared blood-red in the sky in consequence of that preternatural gloom. These were to be understood as tokens of the advent of the day of the Lord, 'that great and notable day,' a day of judgment, to be sure, but more immediately the day of God's salvation to all who invoked His name."

With all respect to such an erudite expositor, however, it is difficult to believe that the startling predictions of Joel were realised in the phenomena accompanying either the crucifixion of Christ or the descent of the Spirit. Surely, if the turning of the sun into darkness and the moon into blood had already happened when Peter quoted the text, he would have said so, and referred explicitly to that solemn sign in heaven. Again, the dramatic character of the prophet's language presages something surpassing any previous sign. While Peter quoted the passage in relation to Pentecost, he unquestionably also looked forward to the end of the "last days" period which Pentecost initiated. "While the lack of perspective in the prophet's vision of the future is universally recognised," says H. L. Ellison, "it is not sufficiently seen that the two comings of our Lord are inseparably connected, two phases of the one divine intervention" (*Men Spake from God*). Joel plainly states that these phenomena are to appear "before the great and terrible day of the Lord come."

His concluding word, however, once more exalts the grace of God above the terrors of His judgments—though the latter are by no means belittled, but predicted in most solemn terms. But, says Joel, "it shall come to pass, that whosoever shall call upon the name of the Lord shall be delivered . . ." Here is the authentic Gospel note; here is new-covenant grace. It is linked, moreover, with God's ultimate purposes for His earthly people, Israel, and the millennial kingdom of Christ. "For in mount Zion and in Jerusalem shall be deliverance, as the Lord hath said, and in the remnant whom the Lord shall call." In his quotation of the final clause of this verse, in Acts 2 : 39, Peter significantly changes the words, "the remnant," to "even as many as the Lord our God shall call." He brings into focus the entire sweep of the redemptive activity of God by His Spirit, from the day of Pentecost, when three thousand were added to the initial band of believers, to the eventual triumph of Israel's Messiah when He shall reign in Jerusalem, great David's greater Son.

5

The Valley of Jehoshaphat

ISRAEL ever cherished the prophetic promise of "the day of the Lord," though they misunderstood what the prophets had to say about it. They thought of it exclusively as the time of divine retribution upon their enemies, and disregarded clear intimations that it would bring judgment upon *themselves* as well as upon their adversaries—indeed, upon all nations. Joel therefore sounds a familiar note in telling what will happen "in those days and at that time . . ." (3 : 1). He links this final section of his book—chapter 4 in the Hebrew Bible—with the concluding part of the preceding chapter, with the conjunction, "*For* behold, in those days . . ." which we have just been considering.

What days they will be! Glorious promises, as well as solemn warnings, are given concerning them. Joel describes them as days when Jehovah will "bring again the captivity of Judah and Jerusalem"—rendered by the *RSV*, "When I restore the fortunes of Judah and Jerusalem." Peter, in his sermon in the temple following the healing of the lame man at the gate called Beautiful, refers to them as "the times of the restitution of all things, which God hath spoken by the mouth of His holy prophets since the world began" (Acts 3 : 21).

Joel does not, however, linger here upon the blessedness of Israel in that day; rather, he proceeds in most sombre terms to tell of the judgment of God upon the nations. Indeed, God Himself speaks directly to them, pronouncing His sentence through the mouth of the prophet. The one who had previously acted as commentator upon current events, now utters the very oracles of God concerning that future day of the Lord. "I will also gather all nations, and bring them down into the valley of Jehoshaphat, and I will enter into judgment with them there" (3 : 2).

The question whether the valley of Jehoshaphat is a place in Palestine, or is to be taken symbolically, is one of the puzzles of Scripture which remain unsolved until the fulfilment of the relevant passages brings complete understanding. The name of Jehoshaphat means "Jehovah judges," and so "the valley of Jehoshaphat" could well signify "the place of God's judgment." Some commentators think there is an allusion to the great victory given to Jehoshaphat over the invading armies of Moab and Ammon, some fifty years before Joel's prophecy—assuming its early date; but the thanksgiving celebration for that victory was held in the valley of Berachah (2 Chron. 20 : 26). Later, the Kidron valley became known as Jehoshaphat's valley, and legend had it that the destruction of Sennacherib's army occurred there. All this, however, is very speculative, and it is preferable to keep to the symbolic meaning of the name. This view is reinforced by the fact that it is termed "the valley of decision" in verse 14.

The chapter contains three clearly defined sections: verses 1–8 tell of judgment upon Israel's neighbouring states and enemies of long standing; verses 9–16, judgment upon "the Gentiles" of all nations; while verses 17–21 describe the felicity of Judah and Jerusalem after these judgments have been executed. The judgment will be based upon the treatment meted out by these nations to "my people and my heritage Israel" (3 : 2). As they have treated Israel, they shall be treated. Our Lord expanded and expounded this principle, in relation to His new-covenant people, in Matthew 25 : 31–46, when He foretold the separation of the "sheep" from the "goats" on the basis of "Inasmuch as ye have done it unto one of the least of these my brethren . . ."

Two important issues are involved in this statement concerning judgment. First, that retribution or reward for "deeds done in the body" is a principle repeatedly affirmed in Scripture. Such a principle is not popular today: retribution has become a banished concept, unworthy of a civilised community. The wrong-doer is not to be punished, but reformed; the naughty child, loved into better ways, not reprimanded. These views of human conduct colour the attitude and teaching of many people concerning God's dealings with mankind. God is love, and so cannot condemn anyone to eternal punishment and outer darkness.

While it may be admitted that our forebears tended to elaborate rather gruesomely upon the torments of hell, we must not evade the fact that Scripture is consistent in its teaching regarding the grave consequences of the rejection of the grace of God in the Gospel, and of retribution for sins of thought, word and deed—unless these are pardoned and blotted out in the precious blood of Christ. We soft-pedal this teaching not only to our own cost, but to the peril of those to whom we preach—whom we should warn and admonish according to the Word.

Secondly, this statement reaffirms, in consonance with all prophetic pronouncements, that Israel is God's chosen, covenant people, His "heritage," despite their unworthiness, disobedience and unbelief. Those who would transfer to the church all the blessings pledged to Israel, do so in defiance of clearest statements that the divine election and calling are "without repentance" (Rom. 11 : 29), and that "God is not a man" to change His mind and transfer His favours (Num. 23 : 19, cf. 1 Sam. 15 : 29). Old Testament and New alike declare that, after the temporary setting aside of Israel for the Gentiles' sake, in this Gospel age, Israel shall be redeemed and restored, at Messiah's coming in power and great in glory to reign on the throne of David.

The charge brought against Israel's neighbouring states is that "they have scattered (my people) among the nations, and parted my land. And they have cast lots for my people; and have given a boy for an harlot, and sold a girl for wine, that they might drink" (3 : 3). This is the conduct of conquerors throughout the ages: the concomitant of war and conquest. It seems, as one reads history, that such acts occur almost unnoticed by God, and incur no penalty. But a day of judgment is coming, when the records will be unrolled, and the consequences of every misdeed will have to be faced. This again is derided teaching today; men think they can "get away with" all kinds of evil. But the Word of God proclaims the certainty of a day of reckoning, when every deed and intent will be taken into account. This is the assurance given to the suffering and the oppressed; the doom pronounced upon all oppressors.

The imagery of the passage is the nonchalant way in which conquerors divided "my land" among themselves; and how they dealt with Israelitish captives: throwing the dice for them, and bartering boys and girls as slaves, for a night's sensual indulgence or a cask of wine.

From His general indictment of the nations, the Lord turns to address the Philistines specifically, and especially Tyre and Zidon, their principal cities. These people had long been bitterly hostile to Israel, and God asks, "Are you paying me back for something?" (3 : 4, *RSV*). Calvin renders this, "'Do I owe anything to you? Am I under any obligation to you? Do ye pay me my recompense?' that is, 'Can you boast of any reason or just pretence for making war on my people?' He then means, that there had been no wrong done to the Tyrians and Sidonians which they could now retaliate, but that they made an attack through their own wickedness, and were only impelled by avarice or cruelty thus to harass the miserable Jews. 'Ye repay not,' he says, 'a recompense to me, for ye cannot pretend that any wrong has been done to you by me.' " Joel proceeds, "If you are paying me back, I will requite your deed on your own head . . ." Rather than being wronged, they had "taken my silver and my gold, and carried my rich treasure into your temples." This included not only sacred vessels from the sanctuary, but plunder from the people. Moreover, they sold the Israelites as slaves to "Grecians"—far-away nations—deliberately to remove them from their land (3 : 6), so that they might seize that land for themselves.

But God would frustrate their intentions, as well as punish their wrongdoing. "I will raise them out of the place whither ye have sold them" (3 : 7). A regathered, restored Israel is part of God's pledged purpose, when He judges the world in righteousness. And He "will requite your deed upon your own head"—again the principle is reiterated, of judgment according to conduct. Unfashionable as this concept is, it is the only satisfactory explanation of the meaning of life, and of the justice of the divine governance. If God is sovereign, then His dispositions of men and nations cannot satisfactorily be explained in terms of their earthly experience. It is only when this life is seen as a probation, as a testing-time for eternity, that it makes sense. It is only when we realise that God keeps eternity ever in view, that we can hold to His utter righteousness as well as His omnipotence.

Men dismiss the Biblical teaching concerning judgment to come, for individuals and nations, as a now outmoded concept. But the people of God have held fast through all generations to the assurance that, in the "day of the Lord," the Judge of all the earth will do right. That is our confidence, based upon the rock of Holy Scripture.

6

Earth's Final Battle

FROM the more limited judgment, upon Israel's neighbours and long-standing enemies (3 : 1–8), Joel turns to address "the Gentiles" in general (3 : 9–16). He does so as the prophet of Jehovah: in this section the Lord does not speak directly through His servant's lips. And his entire message is a summons to battle: "Proclaim ye this among the Gentiles; Prepare war, wake up the mighty men, let all the men of war draw near; let them come up . . ."

This is indeed an awe-inspiring prospect: a world war of unprecedented ferocity. All the efforts of men, all the aspirations of united nations, will not prevent or avoid it. The New Testament in many places augments predictions in the Old, of a final battle involving all the nations of the earth; that Armageddon which shall precede our Lord's appearing. "Beat your plowshares into swords, and your pruninghooks into spears," says Joel, reversing the order of Micah's vision of swords beaten into plowshares during Messiah's reign. The thought is of all resources devoted to the one end, of conducting this war. Moreover, "let the weak say, I am a warrior" (3 : 10). Even those who appear least likely, are drawn into this conflict: here is universal conscription; none can opt out. This will be the ultimate "total war."

"Assemble yourselves, and come, all ye heathen," cries Joel, "and gather yourselves together round about . . . and come up to the valley of Jehoshaphat" (3 : 11–12). While the nations gather to pursue their purposes of evil against Israel in the bitter arbitrament of war, they little realise that they are directed by a higher decree; that they are summoned by God to the place of judgment. These armies are impelled by His sovereign will, albeit their aim is to subjugate His people. They are assembling, if they but knew it, in the valley of Jehoshaphat, the place of divine judgment. Even the most awesome muster of military might is no match for the armies of heaven, and the nations will discover that they are face to face with the Lord God Omnipotent, sitting to "judge all the heathen round about." It is a picture conveying an emphatic implication: the Judge is not an impartial arbitrator ready to hear pleas and to assess arguments: He is enthroned to execute judgment. His sole purpose is to pronounce sentence, and carry it out.

Joel passes from one metaphor to another, in describing the triumph of the Lord over all His enemies, and those of His people. From that of a court of justice, he moves on to that of a harvest-field—a figure of speech adopted by our Lord when describing these same events, to occur at the end of the age (Matt. 13 : 24–30; 36–43): "Put ye in the sickle, for the harvest is ripe . . ." (3 : 13). St. John, in Revelation 14 : 14–18, uses almost identical language to describe the activity of both the Lord Jesus and of attendant angels, at His Advent. Again there is the twofold thought of pronouncing sentence, and carrying it into effect.

The imagery of the harvest is also twofold: the reaping of grain, and the treading out of grapes—"the harvest is ripe; the (wine) presses are full . . ." Both are familiar Scriptural similes for judgment. The "harvest" of sin is fully ripe; the winepress of the wrath of God is full to overflowing with grapes of iniquity, ready for the crushing: "the vats overflow, for their wickedness is great." The suggestion of the language is that, even before the treading of the grapes begins, the wine is flowing through the very pressure of their abundance, and because of their full-ripened state.

At the end of the age will be enacted, upon a universal scale, a judgment which was presaged in miniature by that upon the nations of Canaan at the conquest by Israel. Four hundred years previously Abraham had been told that the land would be given to his progeny, when the iniquity of the Amorites should be full (Gen. 15 : 16). That selfsame metaphor is here applied to all the Gentile nations gathered in the valley of decision.

An awe-inspiring spectacle is presented by the prophetic foreshadowing of things to come: "Multitudes, multitudes in the valley of decision!" The repetition of the word is the Hebrew way of expressing emphasis—vast multitudes: greater, in fact, than the prophet in his day could conceive. And "the valley of decision" does not indicate an indeterminate outcome: Evangelicals have tended to take this phrase out of context, and use it to describe the great majority of people who are undecided in the matter of faith in Christ—the multitudes to whom the Gospel is addressed by evangelists and preachers. The congregations in churches and at missions are described as "in the valley of decision," and are urged to decide aright, for Christ. Such an application is, however, a misuse of the term as it is found here in Joel. These multitudes are not "halting between two opinions" concerning Christ and the Gospel; there is no possibility in this place and at this time, of "deciding for Christ." The day of grace will have run its course; the long period of opportunity ended. The entire burden of the prophecy is that the hour of decisive judgment has come: the day of doom for the ungodly has arrived. Judgment is ready to burst forth.

It is not our purpose to present the whole range of Biblical teaching concerning Armageddon, but only to expound this passage in Joel. The ominous note sounded elsewhere, however, cannot be ignored in any reference to it, and must colour our understanding of these verses.

At this juncture, Joel indicates, his earlier prophecy concerning the sun and moon being darkened, will be fulfilled; and he adds, "the stars shall withdraw their shining" (3 : 15). The terror of the wrath of God is epitomised in the uncanny darkness, and was foreshadowed in the three hours of awesome gloom which shrouded our Saviour on the cross. Isaiah speaks of it thus: "The stars of heaven and the constellations thereof shall not give their light: the sun shall be darkened in his going forth, and the moon shall not cause her light to shine. And I will punish the world for their evil, and the wicked for their iniquity" (Isa. 13 : 10–11); and our Lord on Olivet foretold, "The sun shall be darkened, and the moon shall not give her light, and the stars shall fall from heaven, and the powers of the heavens shall be shaken: and then shall appear the sign of the Son of man in heaven . . ." (Matt. 24 : 29–30).

Then in graphic imagery, the prophet declares that "the Lord shall roar out of Zion"—again, a familiar prediction relating to the Advent. His coming in judgment is repeatedly likened to the roaring of a lion as he springs upon his prey (Isa. 42 : 13; Jer. 25 : 30; Hosea 5 : 14, 11 : 10, 13 : 7–8). Paul puts it more sedately: "The Lord shall descend from heaven with a shout . . ." (1 Thess. 4 : 16).

Very arrestingly, Joel says that "The Lord shall utter His voice *from Jerusalem*"; that is, He shall identify Himself with His people Israel. He shall appear as their Champion, Vindicator, and Deliverer. In fighting against them, the hostile nations have arrayed themselves against the Almighty. At His appearance on the scene, the heavens and the earth shall shake, and all men shall tremble—except His own. To them, "The Lord will be the hope of His people, and the strength of the children of Israel" (3 : 16). Just what that will mean, Joel explains in his concluding verses.

It must always be remembered, in considering this and kindred prophecies, that divine judgment is the concomitant of the outpouring of the Spirit: it is part of the Pentecostal tidings. As H. L. Ellison has already reminded us, "the two comings of our Lord are inseparably connected, two phases of the one great divine intervention." Peter's quotation of this whole passage from Joel, on the day of Pentecost, relates the consummation of the age to the effusion of the Spirit.

It is the commission and delight of the Spirit of God to glorify Christ: to make known, in the Gospel, His saving grace; to draw unto Him all who believe. Pentecost initiated this "day of grace" in which the Gospel is preached. The Gospel becomes, for all who hear it, the determining factor concerning eternal destiny. All are divided into two categories: believers and unbelievers; the redeemed and the unregenerate. To reject or neglect "so great salvation" is to be lost, to come under judgment. God is long-suffering, not willing that any should perish; the Gospel goes out, with its appeal to "whosoever will" to believe and be saved. But the time of opportunity will not be indefinitely extended: the day of judgment is coming. This is the logical sequel to the Pentecostal "dower"; this is the oft-foretold consummation of the age, when the Lord shall see of the travail of His soul and be satisfied.

7

Judah the Joyful

DIVINE judgment, in Scripture, is always seen in twofold aspect: condemnation and punishment of the ungodly and unrepentant, and vindication of trust in God on the part of His own people—of the old covenant and of the new. We should never think of judgment exclusively in terms of the divine wrath upon hardened apostates and unrepentant sinners: that is only one side of the coin. The other is the righting of wrongs experienced by the godly in this life; the establishing of righteousness, and the rewarding of godliness in character and conduct.

For Israel, all the prophets predict ultimate restoration, upon their repentance and recognition of their Messiah; and the fulfilment of promises of unprecedented blessings upon both the people and the land. "All Old Testament prophecy," H. L. Ellison says, "sees in the final setting up of God's kingdom here on a transformed earth the goal of God's purposes." Those who regard the prophecies of material blessing for Israel as conveying in terms of the world we know, the spiritual blessings of the heavenly state for the church of Christ, do violence to the letter and spirit of the Word of God. "The prophets' vision of a transformed earth was not merely the highest that they were capable of comprehending of God's purposes," says Ellison; "it was also the vindication of God's wisdom and purposes in creation."

Joel is therefore in complete accord with all other Old Testament prophets, in foretelling the felicity of Judah and Jerusalem, under the reign of the Lord's Anointed. "So shall ye know that I am the Lord your God dwelling in Zion, my holy mountain: then shall Jerusalem be holy, and there shall no strangers pass through her any more" (3 : 17). The peculiar privilege of Israel—its distinction from all other peoples of the earth—had been this, that the Lord God dwelt in their midst: the shekinah glory in the Holy of Holies in the tabernacle, and later in the temple. The greatest calamity in the long history of the nation occurred when, through their persistent apostasy, the shekinah glory departed, as described by

Ezekiel (10 : 4, 18–19; 11 : 22–23). In the glad "day of restitution" the Lord will again—not now in shekinah glory, but in the Person of the triumphant Christ—dwell in Zion, His "holy mountain."

Jerusalem shall not only enjoy the presence of the Lord, but shall become, for the first time, in fact as well as in name, the holy city. Its iniquity purged, the city and its central shrine—Zion, site of the temple (Isa. 4 : 5; 8 : 18; Jer. 31:6; Mic. 4:7)—shall be "my holy mountain," while all "Jerusalem shall be holy." Holiness is the character of God; and His desire and pattern for His people is that they should be holy. This purpose in its completeness, however, has never been realised, in Israel or in the church; but in the millennial kingdom the glory of His grace will be shown forth in a transformed people, of both old covenant and new. Nothing unclean shall defile; no ugliness of word or deed shall mar relationships; no transgression shall trouble the conscience. Righteousness shall indeed exalt His holy nation.

Moreover Jerusalem, long trodden down by the Gentiles, will be finally at rest from all fear of alarm: "strangers shall never again pass through it." Situate on the historic highway between the great Powers, the city has through the centuries seen the coming and going of countless assailants and contending armies; but no longer will it be trampled under foot by invaders, and its inhabitants will learn the true blessedness of the sacred name *Jehovah-shalom* (Judges 6:24), "the Lord giveth peace."

Then in vision Joel sees the abundance of blessing upon the land, when the ancient description of it as a "land flowing with milk and honey" will be literally fulfilled: "the mountains shall drop down new wine, and the hills shall flow with milk" (3:18). It had been a goodly land when Joshua led the children of Israel into it; but the full blessedness intended by God was withheld because of their failure fully to possess it, and their unworthiness to receive it. Now at long last the ancient promises will be more than wholly realised.

But more important than the temporal benefits will be the spiritual: "a fountain shall come forth of the house of the Lord, and shall water the valley of Shittim." This figure of speech always portrays spiritual blessedness: this "fountain" is identical with Ezekiel's vision of "waters to swim in" (Ezek. 47:1–12), and of John the Divine's vision of the river of water of life (Rev. 22:2). The valley of Shittim is, literally, valley of acacias—which grow only in arid regions—and was situated on the border with Moab. It was the last camping site of the Israelites before they entered

Canaan; a "dry and thirsty place" (*Wycliffe Commentary*), "symbolical of the barrenness and sterility of land where there is no water" (Ellicott). Calvin comments: "Now when the prophet says that waters, flowing from the holy fountain, would irrigate the valley of Shittim, it is the same as though he had said that the blessing of God in Judaea would be so abundant as to diffuse itself far and wide, even to desert valleys."

Amid this anticipation of millennial splendour a harsher note is sounded: further stern condemnation of Egypt and Edom, whose inveterate hatred of Israel, and treacherous treatment of her, seal their doom: "Egypt shall be a desolation, and Edom shall be a desolate wilderness, for the violence against the children of Judah, because they have shed innocent blood in their land" (3:19). It is solemnising to witness today this self-same spirit manifest by the descendants of these ancient enemies of God's chosen race, confirming the decree here pronounced against them.

"But Judah shall dwell for ever, and Jerusalem from generation to generation" (3:20). And Joel's penultimate word tells how this security and felicity shall be sustained: "For I will cleanse their blood that I have not cleansed" (3:21). This is a difficult verse, and commentators differ widely in their interpretation of it. We would suggest, however, that even in the millennial era temptation will not be entirely absent, nor transgression eradicated from His people. But there will be immediate recourse to the fountain opened for sin and all uncleanness; an instantaneous and continuous purging from all defilement.

Some commentators think, however, the promise means that all the entail of past iniquities will be blotted out. Jamieson, Fausset and Brown observe: "I will purge away from Judah the extreme guilt (represented by 'blood,' the shedding of which was the climax of her sin, Isa. 1:15) which was for long not purged away, but visited with judgments (Isa. 4:4). Messiah saves from guilt, in order to save from punishment (Matt. 1:21)." And Calvin writes in similar strain: "We cannot in this place elicit any other meaning than that God will cleanse His church from pollutions; for the prophet no doubt means the defilements of which the people were full . . . Now God, in promising to be a Redeemer, comes to the very fountain and the first thing—that He will wash away their filth; for how could God be the Redeemer of the people, except He blotted out their sin."

More recent scholars, however, tend to translate the Hebrew

word, "avenge," instead of "cleanse" (*RSV*), and *Wycliffe* comments: "the judgment upon the nations will be decisive proof of their guilt and of the innocence of the Jewish victims"—referring back to the judgments upon Egypt and Edom (v. 19). However, that seems to be less relevant than the traditional rendering. In any event, the final clause sets the seal to God's purposes and promises of grace: "for the Lord dwelleth in Zion."

That is the ultimate consummation of the Pentecostal era; the goal to which the Pentecostal effusion was directed. That is the assurance of His people, and the pledge of the fulfilment of all the prophecies, even above all our imaginings, for "eye hath not seen, nor ear heard, neither have entered into the heart of man, the things which God hath prepared for them that love Him" (1 Cor. 2:9).

II

AMOS

THE PEASANT PROPHET

AMOS: JUDAEAN PROPHET TO ISRAEL

Amos is almost as obscure a personage as is Joel. In his case also, all that we know of him is what he reveals in his book; and this is only a little more than Joel says of himself. The few personal particulars which Amos gives, however, are intriguing, and arouse keen interest in him, as a man as well as a prophet. It is hotly debated whether he was a small-scale sheep farmer or a hired shepherd of another's flock. There is good reason for adopting the former view. Another distinctive characteristic of Amos is that he, a Judaean, was sent by God as His messenger to Israel, the northern kingdom. This fact aroused antagonism to his message, as we shall see.

Unlike other prophets, Amos was not a man whose life was devoted to hearing and speaking the Word of the Lord. He was no product of the "schools of prophets," nor a professional "seer." He left his flock for a limited period, at the command of God, to deliver a specific message at Bethel. That done, he presumably returned to his sheep-tending at Tekoa. It is probable that Hosea heard some at least of his oracles, and added God's final word to apostate Ephraim.

I

Setting the Scene

THE personality of Amos has intrigued Bible students perhaps more than that of any other of the minor prophets. This is largely because some of his remarks concerning himself have been misunderstood. His affirmation that he was "no prophet, nor a prophet's son," but rather, "was among the herdmen of Tekoa" and "a gatherer of sycomore fruit," and that "the Lord took me as I followed the flock" (1:1; 7:14–15), was taken to mean that he was of humblest lineage and lowliest occupation—a shepherd who eked out a frugal living as a seasonal fruit-gatherer in summer—or rather "fruit dresser," for the word signifies the pricking of a hard variety of fig (the syc*o*more must not be confused with the syc*a*more trees we know), as an aid to ripening. With this "portrait," however, the felicity and power of his speech, the vivid imagery at his command, and his wide knowledge of the contemporary scene not only in Israel but in other nations, seem incompatible. An added problem lies in the fact that he, an obscure and untaught Judaean peasant, should be sent as God's messenger to the northern kingdom of Israel.

Nothing is known of Amos apart from his own brief observations, just quoted, and what we can deduce from his book as a whole. The dating of his ministry, however—unlike that of Joel—is not seriously disputed. He tells us that the word of the Lord came to him "in the days of Uzziah king of Judah, and in the days of Jeroboam the son of Joash king of Israel" (1 : 1). He mentions Uzziah first, although his prophetic ministry was exercised in Israel, because he was a Judaean and possibly regarded Uzziah—of the house and lineage of David, God's anointed king—as the true king of the entire covenant nation. Although Israel was by far the larger kingdom, and overshadowed Judah, the prophet asserts spiritual priorities and relative relationships as God sees them.

These were times of peak prosperity for both kingdoms. Jeroboam II was an astute soldier-statesman, who exploited a situation favourable to Israel, to its temporary material advantage, though sealing its impending doom through increasingly blatant apostasy. The dominant great Power which threatened the smaller nations of the Middle East, Assyria—which was comparatively soon to wipe Israel out of existence—had devastated Syria, Israel's nearest neighbour and long-standing enemy, and then became distracted by internal troubles, and so was unable for a time to pursue its expansionist ambitions. Jeroboam "made hay while the sun shone," and not only took back from stricken Syria some seized territory, but extended his own borders at Syria's expense. This territorial gain coincided with intensive commercial development. As a major trading route, Israel claimed tolls from all caravans passing through, and also entered upon considerable commercial activities of her own. The consequence was a complete change in the character of the nation's economy. A caste of "merchant princes" sprang up, with great wealth and ostentatiously luxurious living; while agriculture, which had been the backbone of the country's economy, fell into decline. The extremes of opulence among the "tycoons," and poverty in rural areas, is a major theme of the book. The distress of the countryside became acute, as the farmers were increasingly obliged to mortgage their land, and pay crippling rates of interest to oppressive usurers. It was a condition typical of many a greedy "affluent society" in which materialism is predominant, and everything made subservient to its advancement. When spiritual and moral values are subjected to the material, unrighteousness is unleashed and every evil abounds. As it was in Israel then, so it is in the Western world and many other prosperous lands today. That is why Amos has as pertinent a message for us, as for his contemporaries in Samaria and Bethel.

He would have known little or nothing of these facts of the situation, however, had he been merely a herdman of Tekoa—a hireling shepherd, as earlier expositors supposed. More recent research has encouraged the suggestion that Amos was a yeoman farmer, though on a small scale maybe. The word used for "herdman" is not the usual Hebrew word for shepherd, but one which signifies a breeder of a particular variety of desert sheep. He probably had flocks sufficient to necessitate his going to markets in Israel—perhaps to sell his wool—where he would see for himself the state of affairs, and so be sufficiently equipped with information, and roused to indignation concerning the spiritual decline and social injustices of the northern kingdom, to fulfil his prophetic commission.

Thus Amos became, for a limited period, God's prophetic voice to

Israel. He did not choose this rôle, but received it by direct commission from God. Possibly there was no one in Israel at that time equipped for the task; though there were many professional "prophets," they seemingly regarded it as more important to say what would please the king, than to declare the word of the Lord: so this peasant farmer was sent from Judah. Peasant, yes; but by no means ill-educated. His is one of the most colourful books of the Old Testament, and his command of language unexcelled.

Judah, too, was enjoying a brief "Indian summer" under the rule of Uzziah; and, less outrageously ungodly than Israel, its disciplining by Babylonian conquest and exile was farther off. While Amos prophesied in and to Israel, he—like Hosea, shortly afterwards—took sidelong glances at the southern kingdom, and gave warning that God was not regardless of *its* transgressions.

There is sme doubt among expositors regarding the exact date of his ministry: some favour 750 BC; J. K. Howard, in *Among the Prophets*, says that internal evidence points to a date around 755–750 BC; while H. L. Ellison, in *The Prophets of Israel,* adduces cogent reasons for his choice of 763 BC. The interesting suggestion is made by Ellison that the visions of chapters 7–9 constituted the call of Amos to this period of prophetic service; they were given him before he went to Bethel, but he recounted them there as the climax of his three "sermons." Ellison also suggests that the oracles were delivered during the new year (autumn) festival at Bethel, the royal shrine of avowed Jehovah worship, but in fact of degenerate cult practices which had become virtually pagan.

The first word of Amos, after stating his credentials as a prophet, was to declare that the Lord would "roar from Zion, and utter His voice from Jerusalem" (1 : 2). The temple in Jerusalem was His dwelling-place; the shekinah glory between the cherubim in the Holy Place indicated His presence among His chosen people. Although tribal rivalries and dissensions had resulted in the existence of two kingdoms, God did not condone this dichotomy; and although Israel had established its own places of worship, God did not acknowledge them. Yet they were still His covenant people, albeit disobedient; still under obligation to obey His law, and soon to be visited in judgment for their blatant and persistent violation of it.

The very first prophetic word of Amos declared their doom. The strong term "roar," as of a lion about to spring upon his prey, was a familiar prophetic warning of swiftly impending divine judgment. More explicitly Amos proceeded, "the habitations of the shepherds shall mourn, and the top of Carmel shall wither." The rest of the book is an exposition of that terse pronouncement.

Carmel, one of Israel's most sacred sites, was redolent of the nation's history, and particularly of the confrontation between Elijah and the prophets of Baal, when Jehovah, in answering by fire, demonstrated for all time that He is God the Lord. The very name, Carmel, stood for the vindication of God against all the pretensions of false gods and idols; His witness against the apostasy of His people. Not only was Carmel thus an abiding affirmation that Jehovah is the true and living God, but it was also one of the most fertile and fruitful regions in all Palestine—as was testified by its name, which means "green land." No wonder the shepherds would mourn if Carmel were smitten and its pastures withered. If God thus rendered *Carmel* barren, what would happen elsewhere?

The implication of this first figure of speech by Amos would be well understood by a pastoral people; even the merchants would quickly apprehend it, from their earlier familiarity with pastoral metaphors. No matter how propitious their present circumstances might be; no matter how "fat and flourishing" the flocks on Carmel—and fat and flourishing the tradesmen in their prosperous businesses—disaster would come upon them as swiftly and relentlessly as the pounce of a roaring lion upon an overfed lamb. Judgment was imminent. Though it would be executed by Assyria, the overruling hand was the Lord's. This was Israel's eleventh hour.

2

For Three Transgressions and Four

One of the supreme tasks of the Old Testament prophets was to make crystal clear that Jehovah was not merely the God of Israel in the way that the national deities of the heathen nations were the "gods" of those who acknowledged them, but rather was the one true and living God, maker and ruler of heaven and earth. The messages of many of them relate to other peoples as well as Israel; and practically all indicate in one way or another that God's purposes and judgments reach out to all nations. There is therefore nothing remarkable in the fact that Amos begins his book with a series of oracles concerning seven of Israel's neighbouring nations (1:3–2:5). What is noteworthy is his manner of pronouncing these judgments.

Seven short, staccato oracles precede, and lead up to, his main message—one of judgment upon Israel. Like links in a chain, they all open with the solemn declaration, "Thus saith the Lord . . ." Incidentally, the introductory phrases of all this prophet's oracles are significant and striking, as we shall see. Six of these messages of judgment are against heathen nations adjacent to Israel; the seventh against Judah; and the eighth, a shattering indictment of Israel herself. The seven prepare the way for the culminating message.

They gained for Amos a ready, even an eager hearing, as he proclaimed—probably in the market-place, or city gate, the traditional place of civic assembly—the word of the Lord against Israel's long-standing enemies. It was good psychology to begin with Syria, the Philistines, the Phoenicians, Edom, Ammon and Moab; just as Paul in his Epistles began with matters in which he could commend his readers, thus disposing them to heed his exhortations and rebukes, so Amos gained the ear of Israel by condemning their adversaries. There is the added implication that, if God thus judged peoples who had not the benefit of His covenant grace, how could Israel, so greatly privileged, expect to escape the penalty of their sins?

There is in this series of judgments not only a pronouncing of punishment for specific sins, but also a revelation of the character of God's rule in human affairs. Men often behave as if there were no God; nations pursue their policies regardless of His will, heedless even of recognised human standards of moral conduct: and often they seem to achieve their ends. The most brutal aggressors prevail; the most unrighteous men flourish like green bay trees. But the Word of God is consistent in declaring that, contrary to all appearances, they do not really get away with it: there are in heaven records of misdeeds, of men and nations, and ultimately judgment will be meted out by a righteous and omnipotent God.

Commentators through the centuries have been intrigued by the unvarying opening of these eight oracles: "Thus saith the Lord: For three transgressions of . . . and for four, I will not turn away the punishment thereof . . ."—going on to set forth in explicit terms the particular transgressions for which penalty is to be exacted. Some strange speculations have been made concerning the phrase "for three transgressions . . . and for four," but scholars now agree that it is a semitic idiom for repeated transgressions. Thus Moffatt translates it "for crime upon crime." The word rendered "transgressions" means literally "rebellions," *i.e.*, evil deeds, recognised even by heathen peoples as violating the law of God.

The following phrase, "I will not turn away the punishment thereof" is difficult to translate; and the fact that the words "the punishment" are in italics in the *AV* indicates that they are not in the original Hebrew. The *RSV* renders the phrase, "I will not revoke the punishment," but adds a footnote, "Heb., *'cause it to return.'*" The *IVF Commentary* gives, "I will not turn it back," and *Wycliffe*, "I will not intervene." The meaning is clear: the sin of these nations will reap its consequences, unchecked by God. There is a law of cause and effect; of rough justice in the affairs of men and nations: by and large we reap what we sow, unless God in grace intervenes.

In the first seven of the eight messages, also, the punishment is pronounced in identical manner: "I will send (or, kindle) a fire . . ." —a symbol of war. Through the armies of aliens, God would send, or allow, judgment to come upon the evil doers.

This sets the stage for these initial oracles of Amos. The first, against Syria, is addressed specifically to Damascus, the capital city (1:3–5): this was not only the seat of authority, the habitation of the rulers and leaders of the nation, but the centre from which the whole tenor of national life was determined. As Damascus thought and behaved, so did the entire people. The sins condemned in the six heathen nations are invariably cruelties and treachery against neighbouring peoples—in most cases against Israel, stressing as so many prophets do, that conduct toward the covenant people of God is a crucial factor in the divine judgment; but not all are offences against Israel, making clear also that God takes equal heed of all wrong doing, and rules in strict justice. It is *iniquity,* evil conduct in the sight of God and men, the violation of fundamental laws governing human affairs, that God here unequivocally condemns.

The horrors of warfare in those days were indescribable; but the fact that atrocities were almost universally practised did not mitigate the evil of any individual perpetrators. Hazael, king of Syria, and Benhadad, his equally heartless son, should not escape penalty; the bars of the gates of Damascus should be broken—that is, the defences of the city breached; and its inhabitants, who ravaged others, should themselves be subdued and carried away as captives.

The Philistines (1:6–8) were almost extinguished as a distinct people by the time of Amos, but their ancient capital, Gaza, was an abiding reminder of their former barbarities, and especially their active part in the slave trade, selling captive Israelites to Edom. Their long-standing iniquities against the people of God were not forgotten; nor would they be unpunished.

As Gaza was representative of Philistia, so Tyre was of the entire Phoenician race (1:9–10). The ancient "brotherly covenant" between Solomon and Hiram, king of Tyre, is recalled, and the subsequent treachery of Tyre in joining with Gaza in the slave traffic. For this, their city and strongholds should perish.

The enmity between Esau and Jacob persisted, with increasing bitterness, in their progeny, and Edom was through the centuries among the most inveterate of Israel's adversaries (1:11–12). The unrelenting hatred of Edom, already indicated in the judgments upon Gaza and Tyre, is vividly expressed in the graphic phrases—

> . . . he pursued his brother with the sword,
> and cast off all pity,
> and his anger tore perpetually,
> and he kept his wrath for ever . . .

The consequences which Amos foresaw soon came to pass; but the age-old hostility bears evil fruit to this day.

Ammon, descendants of Ben-ammi, son of Lot by his younger daughter (Gen. 19 : 38), were guilty of a particularly bestial practice in war: the murdering of pregnant women in border raids designed to extend their territory. No wonder that Amos seems particularly vehement in uttering sentence upon them—

> fire . . . shall devour her strongholds,
> with shouting in the day of battle,
> with a tempest in the day of the whirlwind . . .

Moab, descendants of the son of Lot by his elder daughter (Gen. 19:37), is condemned for an offence, not against Israel, but against Edom—Israel's bitter foe; but nevertheless a shameful crime against humanity (2:1–3). The desecration of a corpse was regarded as sacrilege in the ancient world. This particular instance, of "burning the bones of the King of Edom into lime," is otherwise unrecorded in history, but not in the records of heaven. Fire, by which Moab desecrated these royal bones, should "devour the strongholds of Merioth," and Moab's king and princes should pay the penalty for the evil deed.

Six oracles of judgment upon unfriendly heathen nations would evoke nods of approbation from the prophet's hearers; but when he went on to speak in similar terms of Judah, Israel's sister-nation—albeit there was occasional tension and even conflict between them—his words came nearer home (2:4–5). And remember, this oracle was uttered by a man of Judah, to the people of Israel. One can imagine a stiffening of the stance and tautening of the faces of his audience as he uttered the now-familiar terms of indictment against *Judah*. How essential it was, however, in the chain of cumulative judgments, that Judah should be included; for had it not been so, Amos might have been accused of tribal jealousy; of blindness to the faults of his own people, while reproving Israel's. It was also a premonitory warning that the message of the prophet was not merely condemnatory of alien nations, but was coming right home to the covenant people of God.

But the manner of the charge is altered: Judah is not accused of crimes against humanity, but of ignoring the law of the Lord, and disobeying His commandments. It did not cite specific sins, but was an arraignment for apostasy. The covenant God of Israel (using that term of the entire nation, including Judah) was indicting them for defection from the terms of the covenant. Generation after generation had been "led astray by lies" (*i.e.*, had worshipped false gods); instead of walking in the steps of their father Abraham, of David and other godly kings, they preferred the evil precepts and practices of those who beguiled them into apostasy and idolatry. Therefore "I will send fire upon Judah, and it shall devour the palaces of Jerusalem." That penalty, fulfilled in the destruction of the city by Nebuchadnezzar, was still far off: its pronouncement, however, prepared the way for the message of more immediate doom upon Israel, which was the main burden of the ministry of Amos.

3

Social and Spiritual Ills

For the eighth time Amos uttered the portentous words, "Thus saith the Lord . . ." as he began his arraignment of Israel (2:6–16). The first charges against them, significantly, are in the same category as those against the heathen nations—social unrighteousnesses—rather than apostasy from God, as in the case of Judah: but this more serious indictment is soon to follow. The sin particularised in the initial accusation, however, is that the rich and powerful in Israel "sold the righteous for silver, and the poor for a pair of shoes."

This is staggering: surely far more heinous sins than these could be cited against Israel? According to our assessment, maybe; but the fact that these misdeeds against fellow human beings are given priority in the Lord's condemnation of Israel emphasises how seriously He regards deliberate offence against human personality: and particularly those against fellow Israelites—or, in new covenant times, fellow believers.

The sin envisaged here is that manipulation of the law by which a poor man was sold into slavery for debt. "The law allowed a poor man to sell himself into slavery (Lev. 25:39; Deut. 15:12), but it did not sanction the sale of an insolvent debtor, which is evidently what is meant here (2 Kings 4:1; Neh. 5:5). The poor man was sold 'for a pair of shoes' (v. 6), or 'for an old song,' as we might say," observes the *IVF Commentary*. These greedy Israelites even begrudged the distressed debtor the handful of dust he would, according to the custom of the day, throw over his head to express his misery: they "pant after the dust of the earth on the head of the poor"—though the *RSV* gives a different turn to this phrase:

> they trample the head of the poor into the
> dust of the earth . . .

Such predatory, heartless iniquity has been perpetrated by avaricious oppressors of the poor in all races, in all generations. Among professing people of God, it is most grievous. Tyrants of this sort preen themselves upon their astute methods of gaining both possessions and power: they little think that One much greater and more powerful than they will call *them* to account.

This is a solemnising thought in our day, when certain evil men exploit, dominate, brain-wash and enslave not only individuals, but entire nations. On a large or smaller scale, however, violation of personality will meet its penalty.

The second count in the indictment of Israel follows swiftly on the heels of the first. These rapacious rich people "turn aside the way of the meek"—or "the afflicted" (*RSV*), probably meaning the denial of justice in the courts. Some commentators, in fact, suggest that the whole passage refers to the corruption of judges, who could be "bought" by so small a bribe as a pair of shoes. When evil men occupy positions of authority, and godly principles are set aside, debased standards infect every sphere of life. This is the blight which follows the abandonment of regard for righteous conduct.

Again, we should do well to heed the implications of this admonition by Amos. Even more relevant to our present situation in the western world, however, is the fact that this state of affairs is the bitter fruit of selfish materialism. The stern condemnation of Israel contains pertinent warning for our materialistic generation.

Such departure from upright standards of conduct is always accompanied by licentiousness and immorality. In the case of Israel, "a man and his father go in to the same maiden . . ." (2:7). This alludes to the Canaanite practice of "sanctuary prostitution," adopted by the Israelites in their apostasy, at their shrines and "high places"; but the divine condemnation applies equally to immorality of all kinds. On the part of professing people of God it is particularly offensive, for thereby "my holy name is profaned." Worst of all, however, is the perpetration of evil and idolatrous practices *in the name of God*; pretending that these are condoned by Him, and even acceptable as acts of worship. So disastrously, however, can apostate people deceive themselves.

When religion becomes a cloak or excuse for sensual indulgence, there are no lengths to which its devotees will not go—"they lay themselves down beside every altar upon garments taken in pledge" —*i.e.*, forfeited pledges; and "in the house of their God they drink the wine of those who have been fined" (2:8). It would seem that wine for these orgies was provided from money exacted in the courts as fines. To such depths of depravity had both the civil and religious life of the nation descended. While not suggesting that such conditions as these prevail in the western world today, nevertheless much is done in the name of God which He utterly repudiates in His Word and condemns by His prophets; and alas, thereby reproach is brought upon His holy name.

From condemnation of these social iniquities and sins of apostasy, the Lord goes on to express through Amos His indignation at the adoption by Israel of these idolatrous and evil ways of the very Canaanites He subdued before them, and whose land He gave them. Strong and powerfully entrenched as the Amorites were, He gave Israel victory over them. Earlier still, He had brought His people out of the slavery of Egypt; led and provided for them forty years in the wilderness; and given them possession of the promised land (2:9–10). Nor was Israel's present decadence due to any failure on God's part to instruct and inspire them: He raised up prophets, to indicate His will and admonish concerning His way; and Nazirites —ordinary "laymen" desirous of expressing their devotion to the Lord and zeal for His law—to challenge and encourage others by their example of dedication and devotion. But the prophets were silenced, by many and devious means; and the Nazirites, abhorred for their "fanaticism," were seduced and made drunk—thus violating their vows (2:11–12).

To oppose the truly godly; to stifle their witness for God and His truth; to deride them as fanatics, is the unvarying reaction of the ungodly—and it evokes the divine wrath in the New Testament as emphatically as in the Old. Luke solemnly records that Herod the Tetrarch, that man of many evil deeds, "added yet this above all, that he shut up John in prison" (Luke 3:20); and in silencing the voice of God's final messenger to him, he sealed his own doom. Our Lord Jesus, brought before Herod during His series of mock "trials," had no word at all to say to him. The silence of the Saviour was more terrible than the most severe reproach or reproof: it indicated that God's final word to that condemned soul had been spoken.

Indictment; then production of the evidence and proving of the charge, are followed by the pronouncing of sentence (2 : 13–16). Amos uses three graphic metaphors to bring home to his hearers the penalty they are to pay. First, "I will press you down . . . as a cart full of sheaves presses down" (*RSV*). To an agricultural people, this would be a vivid figure of speech. Howard's rendering is even more striking: "I will crush you as the sheaves of corn are crushed beneath the threshing wagon . . ." There is, however, difference of interpretation concerning this phrase, for the Hebrew text is obscure. The *AV* renders it, "Behold, I am pressed under you, as a cart is pressed that is full of sheaves" (2 : 13). If this is the true meaning of the verse, then it expresses the travail of Jehovah through the sins of His people. "Here is a perception," observes one recent commentator, "that truly anticipates the cross." The majority of scholars, however, favour the rendering of the *RSV*, quoted above.

The second metaphor is this: "Flight shall perish from the swift, and the strong shall not retain his strength, nor the mighty save his life" (2 : 14). Capacity for self-defence in warfare shall fail in Israel; the bravest and best of her warriors shall be powerless against their adversaries in the day of retribution; and the fleetest of foot unable to escape.

Moreover, "He who handles the bow shall not stand; and he who is swift of foot shall not save himself, nor he who rides the horse save his life; and he who is stout of heart among the mighty shall flee away naked in that day, says the Lord" (2 : 15–16). And thus it came to pass in the Assyrian invasion; equally certain is the fulfilment of every prophetic word of the Lord.

4

A Prophet's Questionnaire

In his first brief oracle against Israel (2:6–16) Amos in effect said all that he had to declare in the name of the Lord. He enunciated the divine allegations, and stated plainly what the consequences of their sins would be. It is consonant with the character of God, however, and the experience of all the prophets, that Amos was not content to discharge this responsibility and then adopt the attitude, "Well, if you won't pay attention, that's your lookout!" The repeated warnings and admonitions of the prophets, until the very hour of judgment, indicate the longsuffering of the Lord; His reluctance to condemn and willingness to forgive even unto the last moment, if only they would repent and turn to Him. And so Amos, in further "sermons," spells out in more detail the various aspects of the terse yet far-reaching message he has already given.

We have observed the arresting manner in which Amos begins his oracles. Having proclaimed, "Thus saith the Lord . . ." eight times, like the tolling of a solemn bell, he now rings the changes by opening three pronouncements with the challenge, "Hear this word . . ." (3 : 1; 4 : 1; 5 : 1), and for good measure throws in one more "Hear ye . . ." (3: 13). God had spoken, and was speaking still; it behoved Israel to hearken, and to obey. If they had done so, their subsequent history would have been very different from what the prophet foretold—but which, alas, all too tragically came to pass.

The first of these three utterances is addressed to "the whole family which I brought up from the land of Egypt . . ." (3 : 1). Although Amos was prophesying in, and primarily to, Israel, he makes clear that the Lord regards the entire nation, the "children of Israel," as still His covenant people. Their division into two kingdoms was a tragic schism between brethren; a rending apart of one family. For not only were they blood-brothers, but together they constituted His chosen race—"You only have I known of all the families of the earth" (3:2). The word rendered "known" is often used in Scripture of the marriage relationship; and that in its turn is used by God as a figure of speech for His relationship with Israel. The entire nation is sharply reminded that, although sundered by rivalries and jealousies, both kingdoms are alike in guilt before God, and they will be punished according to the privileges and opportunities given to them—"therefore I will punish you for all your iniquities."

Then the prophet authenticates his own ministry as Jehovah's spokesman in a most striking manner. He asks a series of questions somewhat reminiscent of the extended and penetrating "divine questionnaire" to Job, which reduced that patriarch to awed submission. The questions of Amos, however, all illustrate the law of cause and effect: certain actions have inevitable consequences—and if those consequences occur, then the reason for them is clear and plain. And the reason for these prophecies of Amos was that the compulsion of the Spirit of God lay behind the words he uttered—

> Do two walk together,
> unless they have made an appointment?
> Does a lion roar in the forest,
> when he has no prey?
> Does a young lion cry out from his den,
> if he has taken nothing?
> Does a bird fall in a snare on the earth,
> when there is no trap for it?
> Does a snare spring up from the ground,
> when it has taken nothing?
> Is a trumpet blown in a city,
> and the people are not afraid?

When two people set out on a walk together, it may be assumed that they have arranged to do so; it doesn't just happen fortuitously. A lion doesn't roar unless he has something to roar about! A bird doesn't get caught in a snare unless it is baited and set; and the trap doesn't jerk upward unless a bird has "sprung" it. A city watchman doesn't sound an alarm unless an enemy is approaching. Behind all these acts lies an impelling cause.

These illustrations are in the realm of the everyday experience of the people whom Amos was addressing; then he lifts the discourse on to a higher plane, introducing the thought of the sovereignty of God in human affairs—

> Does evil befall a city,
> unless the Lord has done it?

In the issues affecting His people and His land, God rules and over-rules: His purposes surely come to pass. The Assyrian invasion which Amos foretold was ordained and directed by *their* covenant God.

The cumulative impact of this questionnaire must have been extremely powerful in emphasising the fact that certain events follow one another as night follows day. Amos then abruptly makes the affirmation, "Surely the Lord God does nothing without revealing His secret to His servants the prophets" (3:7), and drives home his point in two further devastating questions—

> The lion has roared;
> who will not fear?
> The Lord God has spoken,
> who can but prophesy?

This is the climax to which he has been leading; the conclusive logic of his chain of argument; he, a man of Judah, was prophesying in Israel because he could do no other. God had spoken in his soul, and now gave utterance through his lips. It was not he, Amos, herdman of Tekoa, pronouncing condemnation upon Israel, but Adonai Jehovah. As His prophet, Amos could do no other than speak. "The passage 3 : 3–8," says Ellison, "is primarily a vindication of Amos' right to prophesy, but it is far more. It affirms that God's dealings with men follow consistent principles, which at least in general outline are understandable by men."

The prophet then dramatically envisages a summons to Philistia and to Egypt, heathen peoples to the north and to the south, to witness the internal convulsion occasioned by the social injustices in Israel, "for they know not how to do right"—they have lost all sense of moral standards; and by their iniquities they "store up violence and robbery in their strongholds" (3 : 9–10). We know only too well in our own day that these social turmoils inevitably ensue upon exploitation and oppression; and human nature was much the same in ancient Israel as it is now in the west. Philistia and Egypt (or, as some scholars think, Assyria and Egypt: the Hebrew is obscure) are thus invited to come and see what is happening in Samaria, "so that when the hour of doom arrives they may agree that justice, and only justice, has been done," says Ellison. How characteristic of God to observe His own law that two witnesses should be essential to the execution of judgment!

Taking advantage of Israel's decadence and disunity, "An enemy shall surround the land; and he shall bring down thy strength" (3 : 11). The savagery of the Assyrian assault is foretold in an almost terrifying metaphor: "As the shepherd taketh out of the mouth of the lion two legs, or a piece of an ear; so shall the children of Israel be taken out that dwell in Samaria in the corner of a bed, and in Damascus in a couch" (3 : 12). Like a lion indeed, the Lord "roared," and like a lion Assyria tore and devoured its prey, so that only a pitiable, lifeless residue was left. This savaged remnant, intermingling and intermarrying with the heathen immigrants brought in by conquerors to populate the land, became in course of time the despised Samaritans of whom we read in Ezra and Nehemiah, and onward into the days of our Lord.

The allusion to Damascus has puzzled Bible students: some suggest that this is a confirmation of the judgment upon Syria; others, that the term really means "Damascus-cloth"—so that the *RV* renders the phrase, "on the silken cushions of a bed," and *RSV*, "so shall the people of Israel who dwell in Samaria be rescued, with the corner of a couch and part of a bed." The *IVF Commentary* observes, "The whole picture is one of utter wretchedness for the few survivors of Samaria."

As if to accentuate the solemnity and authority of his words, Amos repeats the adjuration, "Hear ye, and testify in the house of Jacob, saith the Lord God, the God of hosts . . ." (3 : 13). There is, however, some difference of opinion regarding the interpretation of this verse. *Ellicott's Commentary* suggests that this command is addressed, not to Israel, but "to the foreign nations Egypt and Philistia referred to in v. 9," and Jamieson, Fausset and Brown add, "God calls the heathen Philistines and the Egyptians to witness with their own eyes Samaria's corruptions above described, so as that none may be able to deny the justice of Samaria's punishment." The traditional view, however, is succinctly stated by Matthew Henry: "Notice is given of it (*i.e.*, God's judgment) to themselves (v. 13). Let this be *testified*, and *heard*, *in the house of Jacob*, among all the seed of Israel, for it is spoken by *the Lord God*, *the God of hosts*, who has authority to pass this sentence and ability to execute it."

To whomsoever the command was spoken, however, Amos proceeds to spell out the full scale and scope of the impending judgment. "In the day that I shall visit the transgressions of Israel upon him I will also visit the altars of Bethel: and the horns of the altar shall be cut off, and fall to the ground . . ." (3 : 14). The debased religion of the nation will be destroyed with it: the place of sacred association in the past, degraded into a centre for idolatrous ritual and sensual indulgence, will be devastated. The altars, no longer places of true worship of Jehovah, of confession and repentance and sacrifice unto Him, are to be overthrown, disowned and disgraced, and their "horns"—projecting points at the corners of the altar on which the blood of offerings was sprinkled—cut off. All this signifies a complete shattering of the shrine at Bethel, and an ending of religious practices associated with it. There may also be an allusion to the fact that the altar was a place of refuge, if a fugitive should lay hold on its horns. There will be no place of refuge and escape from *this* Avenger!

The final word in this oracle depicts the similarly total destruction of the palatial homes of the ruling caste and the *nouveaux riches*: "And I will smite the winter house with the summer house; and the houses of ivory shall perish, and the great houses shall have an end, saith the Lord" (3 : 15). The opulence of the oppressors of the poor shall not save them: they will not be able to buy exemption from the all-embracing devastation wrought by the invaders. Their luxurious town and country houses will all be ravaged; indeed, in stark and simple words the spokesman of Jehovah declares that everything the unrighteous rulers and unscrupulous financiers had so cruelly grasped, "shall have an end." When that is God's last word, it is conclusive indeed.

5

Kine of Bashan

KEY-NOTE of the second of the three discourses of Amos beginning with "Hear this word . . ." (4:1–13) is in the phrase, repeated like a refrain, "Yet have ye not returned unto me, saith the Lord" (4 : 6, 8, 9, 10, 11). The prophet reminds the people of Israel of the means by which the Lord had sought to constrain them unto repentance and returning to Him: yet they resisted His every effort—with inevitable consequences.

Amos had already indicated the bounty of God in blessings upon Israel: He gave them victory over their enemies, and possession of the land (2 : 9–11). In their apostasy, He sent chastisements to check their waywardness and lead them to renewal of their vows (4 : 6–11). But alas, blessing and chastisement alike were unavailing: they remained unrepentant and unresponsive. Inevitably a "therefore" follows: because of their persistence in rejection of His grace, the threatened judgment will surely ensue (4 : 12–13).

Earlier in the chapter, however, Amos addresses the rich women of Samaria, in terms of most scathing sarcasm. Often the prophets recognise the responsibilitiy of women as at least equal to that of men, for the state of affairs in the nation. The men would have been slow to acknowledge this, for women were regarded as dutiful dependants, without personal status or influence. It was the popular fiction among the menfolk that women were mere appendages to the lords of creation; a reflection of their authority and glory. The Bible is more realistic than that, however: it frankly portrays the powers which some women possess to persuade and cajole, deceive and dominate their fathers, husbands and sons. Then, as now, some women ruled the roost; and others revelled in the luxuries which they well knew to be acquired by the evil practices of their menfolk. They condoned, if they did not actively inspire or participate in the oppression of the poor; they fully shared their husbands' guilt.

In unflattering terms, Amos speaks of them as "kine of Bashan" (4 : 1): pampered cattle, basking in the enjoyment of "the fat of the land." Bashan was renowned for its rich pasture-lands; it was to

Israel what the Rye and Romney marshes are to South-East England: superb fattening-grounds. Its herds were the sleekest in the country. Fit symbols of these self-indulgent women! Such luxury-loving people did not care what privation others might suffer, so long as they were able to indulge their every whim. Indeed, they "crush the needy," and "say to their husbands, 'Bring, that we may drink!'" (4 : 1).

Their heartless greed brought upon them the wrath of God, however, who "has sworn by His holiness"— that is, by Himself; His character and affronted righteousness—that calamity shall swiftly come upon them. The invaders, Amos declares, "shall take you away with hooks, and your posterity (*i.e.*, your daughters) with fish-hooks" (4 : 2). This terrible doom most likely came literally to pass, for Assyrian monuments depict strings of captives led by means of hooks through their noses or mouths. These women of Samaria would be led through breaches in the battered city walls (4 : 3); and they would be cast . . . where? " . . . into the palace," says the *AV*; "into Harmon," says *RSV*. In fact, the Hebrew is so obscure that no one knows precisely what Amos said, and we must be content with the observation of the *IVF Commentary*, "In any case, some unpleasant fate is indicated."

Under the very shadow of such terrors, the people of Israel pursued their valueless religious ritual, and with biting sarcasm Amos derides them: "Come to Bethel, and transgress; at Gilgal multiply transgression: and bring your sacrifices every morning, and your tithes . . ." (4 : 4–5). By means of stinging irony, the prophet attempts to stab them awake to the folly and uselessness of their punctilious religious exercises: these have no other effect than to gratify their own whims and religious inclinations—"for so you love to do, O people of Israel!"

From ridicule Amos turns to straightforward, stark condemnation, in a series of five reminders of specific chastisements sent by God in endeavour to check them in their wayward course—each ending with the key-phrase, "Yet you did not return to me, says the Lord."

The first chastisement was famine: "I have given you cleanness of teeth, and want of bread . . ." (4 : 6). Secondly, the withholding of rain—one of the penalties specifically foretold by Moses, before Israel entered the land, if they should "turn aside and serve other gods" (Deut. 11 : 17). So markedly were these drought conditions related to the spiritual state of the people, that there had been rain in one city and not in another; upon one field and not upon another

(4 : 7). And it had been unavailing for the people in the not-rained-upon city to stagger—for that is the force of the Hebrew word—to the one which had rain, because even there "they were not satisfied" (4 : 8): the inhabitants of the city could not spare water for strangers, from their scanty supplies. Thirdly, blight and mildew and locusts devastated the fields, vineyards and gardens (4 : 9). Fourthly, plague "after the manner of Egypt," and defeat in battle decimated the nation (4 : 10). Finally, through earthquake or similar "natural" disaster, "as when God overthrew Sodom and Gomorrah," many lost their lives, and those who escaped did so as by a miracle—"Ye were as a firebrand plucked out of the burning" (4 : 11). All these calamities, forecast by Moses as consequences of apostasy, "if thou wilt not hearken unto the voice of the Lord thy God, to observe all His commandments and statutes which I command thee . . ." (Deut. 28 : 15–48), had come upon them.

Through these varied and manifest judgments of God, the people of Israel remained obdurate in their hardness of heart; unyielding in their impenitence. Therefore judgment should come upon them which would be, not remedial, but retributive. In stern summons Israel is exhorted, "Prepare to meet thy God!" (4 : 12). The Omnipotent Creator of the worlds, the Omniscient Maker of mankind, the Omnipresent Jehovah, the God of hosts, is about to effect His final judgement upon His guilty people, Israel.

6

Lamentation over Israel

AMOS himself entitles his third "Hear this word . . ." discourse as a lamentation over Israel (5 : 1). Ellison considers it a "funeral lament." The prophet bewails the utter vanquishing of the nation, indeed its virtual extinction, at the hands of the Assyrians. Although that event was still future, Amos describes it as already accomplished, so certainly would it come to pass. This use of the "prophetic past" tense for events which were in fact still future is common with the prophets, in order to bring home to the people the urgency of the warning concerning the catastrophic judgments toward which they were hastening. There could be no escaping the consequences of their sin: these were already determined, "signed, sealed and delivered" in the purposes of God—but always with one proviso: true repentance, honest and earnest turning to God would avert the disaster and evoke His forgiving grace, even at the very last moment. That note of urgent warning, admonishment and entreaty runs through this chapter, as through every such message of every prophet.

Amos proclaims that "the virgin of Israel is fallen; she shall no more rise: she is forsaken upon her land; there is none to raise her up" (5 : 2). The Lord often likens Israel to a virgin, whom He espoused to Himself in the wilderness. It was His own covenant people who had so violated their espousals that He had no other recourse than to cast them off. Some commentators, however, see in the word "virgin" an allusion to the fact that the kingdom of Israel had never before been subjugated by an invader (*Wycliffe*). The contrast between her unconquered past and impending overthrow is thus accentuated.

The prophet goes on to describe the total rout of Israel's armies; nine out of every ten of its men would be slain (5 : 3). The very thought of this terrible nine-fold decimation melts the heart of the prophet, and he breaks forth in anguished entreaty: "Thus saith the Lord unto the house of Israel, Seek ye me, and ye shall live" (5 : 4). It is love's supreme effort; the further constraint of divine grace upon the minds and hearts of a people blind and besotted in their wilful apostasy. The prophet re-emphasises, however, the need for reality, for sincerity in seeking the Lord: it is *He* to whom they must turn, not to their religious ritual—"But seek not Bethel, nor enter into Gilgal, and pass not to Beer-sheba . . ." (5 : 5). Their debased religious shrines and practices were doomed, whether the people repented or not: there could be no hope in relying upon them: "for Gilgal shall surely go into captivity, and Bethel shall come to nought." Every trace of the degraded religion which had displaced the true worship of Jehovah would be blotted out. God has no room or pity for false faith; for that which deceives and deludes people into thinking they are right with God when their lives are in flagrant contradiction to His will.

The one way of escape from judgment lay in a true turning to God. "Seek *the Lord* and ye shall live" (5 : 6). This is the authentic note of all the law and the prophets—that to be religious is not necessarily to be godly, but rather may blind the "worshipper" to the real facts of his condition and condemnation before God. God is not to be bought or bribed by the offering of sacrifices or solemn services: He demands obedience to His word and will, worship in spirit and truth, and conformity of life to the profession made in His presence. So, Amos urges, "Seek the Lord . . . lest He break out like a fire in the house of Joseph, and devour it, and there be none to quench it in Bethel."

He then specifically addresses those who pervert justice to their own ends; who "turn judgment to wormwood . . ." (5 : 7). Wormwood, a poisonous herb, was proverbial for bitterness in speech, action or experience. "Few things can be more bitter," observes the *New Bible Commentary*, "than the award of a corrupt court." Even such people as these, however, were not beyond the reach of redeeming grace: so Amos pleads with them to seek "Him that maketh the seven stars of Orion . . ." (5 : 8). The book of Job had familiarised the people of Israel with the thought of God as the One "which maketh . . . Orion and Pleiades . . ." (Job 9 : 9), the Almighty, the only true God and creator of heaven and earth. All these expressed and exemplified His unchangeable character: the God of righteousness and truth. Could anything be too hard for Him—even the pardoning and restoring of sinners such as these?

The words "Seek Him" at the beginning of v. 8, in the *AV*, are in italics, indicating that they are not in the original. Most commentators describe verses eight and nine as a doxology; and some suggest that it is displaced here, from the end of chapter 4. There is no evidence to support such a transposition, however; rather, the verses exalt most fittingly the One whom Israel is implored to seek. Jehovah their God is the only true and living God; and in all the affairs of men He is working His purposes out. The issues of life and death are in His hand; and, says Amos, He "strengtheneth the spoiled against the strong"—upholding the righteous and oppressed, and bringing calamity upon the oppressors, so that "destruction comes upon the fortress." Whatever "stronghold" they resort to, will be overthrown. "God's irresistible power destroys that which is the basis of human pride" (*Wycliffe*).

Alas, Amos testified and entreated in vain. "They hate him that rebuketh in the gate, and they abhor him that speaketh uprightly" (5 : 10). The city gate was the focal centre of civic life and activity. Here was the court of justice, so called (cf. v. 7); business was transacted here; and it was also the popular market-place. Not unnaturally, the prophets usually proclaimed the word of the Lord at the city gate; and here, probably, Amos delivered his discourse.

He returns to specific accusations against the oppressors of the poor (5 : 11), who with their ill-gotten gains built themselves substantial stone houses and pleasant vineyard-gardens. But, warned the prophet, they would not live for very long in the houses, nor enjoy wine from the vineyards: all these would be swept away by the Assyrian holocaust. "For I know your manifold transgressions and your mighty sins," says the Lord (5 : 12). They dealt deviously with the poor, and bribed the magistrates to condone their iniquities. So perverted were the times that even those who personally held to higher standards turned a blind eye upon the prevailing evils—"the prudent keep silence at such a time." No wonder Amos sums up his indictment, "It is an evil time!" (5 : 13).

In inspired endeavour to overcome evil with good, however, he makes a further appeal: "Seek good, and not evil, that ye may live . . ." (5 : 14–15). Even now it was not too late for individuals to dissociate themselves from their "evil and perverse generation" and to seek the Lord: for "it may be the Lord God of hosts will be gracious unto the remnant of Joseph." By using the evocative name of Joseph, the prophet recalls that illustrious forebear and his steadfast allegiance to the Lord. God, who was gracious to Israel for their fathers' sakes, had also repeatedly promised to fulfil His purposes through a faithful remnant. They, to whom Amos was appealing, could be among that remnant.

Returning to his lament, the prophet envisages "wailing in all the streets (of towns and cities), and in all the highways (of rural areas)." The despairing cry of the few survivors of the Assyrian assault wrings the heart of the prophet—and of the Lord: nevertheless it is *He* who will pass through the land in judgment, by means of the Assyrians. This disabuses their minds of mistaken notions concerning that oft-foretold "day of the Lord." While this term is found three times in Joel (1 : 15; 2 : 1, 11), this use of it by Amos was the first time any prophet in Israel had specifically employed it. However, as Ellison well says, "it is obvious that the prophet is speaking of a concept well known to his hearers." They had disregarded, however, what had been clearly indicated concerning it, and preferred to think of this "day" as a demonstration of the superior status and strength of Jehovah their God over the gods of their adversaries. In a display of His greater authority and might than theirs, He would give His people overwhelming victory over those who served other gods. He would vindicate and consolidate His own station, they foolishly thought, by exalting those who "worshipped" Him, and subduing their enemies.

Oh, no! said Amos. The day of the Lord would see the vindication of righteousness and truth, and the subduing of evil among His own people first and foremost. For them in their apostasy it would be a "day of darkness, and not light" (5 : 18). There would be no escaping the stroke of His judgment upon *them*, albeit they were Israelites—"As if a man did flee from a lion, and a bear met him; or went into a house, and leaned his hand on a wall, and a serpent bit him" (5 : 19). And to underline his prediction Amos repeats, "Shall not the day of the Lord be darkness, and not light? even very dark, and no brightness in it?" (5 : 20).

The discourse reaches its culmination with a stinging, scornful rejection by God of their attempts to ingratiate themselves with Him by religious ritual; to bribe Him with sacrifices and offerings—"I hate, I despise your feast days, and I will not smell in your solemn assemblies. Though ye offer me burnt-offerings and your meat-offerings, I will not accept them . . ." (5 : 22). Sacrifices and offerings had been ordained and established by God as a means of approach to Him; an expression of reverential worship. But, divorced from a right relationship of heart and mind with Him, and conformity of life to His will, these became not only valueless but abhorrent to God. Likewise the uplifting of heart and voice in His praise is glorifying to God when it is rendered in sincerity: He invites His people to bring "the sacrifice of praise . . . that is, the fruit of our lips giving thanks to His name" (Heb. 13 : 15). But if it is devoid of the love of our hearts and the loyalty of our lives, He commands, "Take thou away from me the noise of thy songs; for I will not hear the melody of your music" (5 : 23). His requirements are clear and plain: "Let judgment run down as waters, and righteousness as a mighty stream" (5 : 24). Since Israel had failed to observe and practise these, God would exemplify them toward Israel in His overwhelming visitation.

There had been a time when, in the wilderness, His people had offered acceptable sacrifices to the Lord: when these expressed a right attitude toward and relationship with Him (5 : 25). They therefore could not plead ignorance of His requirements, or inability to fulfil them. But they preferred their sinful ways and indulgences; their idolatry, to walking with the Lord in the light of His word. "Ye have borne the tabernacle of your Moloch and Chiun your images, the star of your god, which ye made to yourselves" (5 : 26). There is some obscurity about this verse, however; the *RSV* reads, "You shall take up Sakkuth your king, and Kaiwan your star-god, your images, which you made for yourselves." *Wycliffe Commentary* observes, "It is impossible at the present time to identify Sakkuth. Kaiwan was a Babylonian god sometimes identified with Saturn." Howard, on the other hand, declares them to be "two Assyrian deities" (so also *IVF*), and adds that Amos, "in reminding Israel of the doom that is at hand, points out that she will soon be languishing in exile in the land of her erstwhile gods."

The *IVF Commentary* gives the verse a different implication, however: "By her sin and evil ways Israel had, by implication, made the Assyrian gods her own. The prophet visualises captivity in Assyria, *beyond Damascus* (5 : 27). She would presently take up these idols in the land of her captivity, and so make explicit what before has only been implicit."

Whichever view is correct, the implication for Israel was unmistakable: conquest by Assyria, and being carried away into captivity was the penalty of their sin, the consequence of their idolatry. The Lord of hosts had determined and spoken it.

It is significant that Stephen, quoting Amos 5 : 25–27 in his address before the Sanhedrin, (Acts 7 : 42–43) gives a slightly differing rendering, from the LXX text. This implies that the idolatry which reached its peak in the final days of the northern kingdom and in Jerusalem before its destruction by Nebuchadnezzar, was the full flowering of a root reaching back to the golden calf made during the wilderness wanderings. A full and illuminating discussion of the implications of the adaptation by Stephen of the quotation from Amos, will be found in the commentary on *Acts* by Prof. F. F. Bruce, in the *New London Commentary* series.

7

At Ease in Zion

THERE is really no break between chapters five and six of Amos; the latter is a continuation of his lamentation over Israel. This fact is emphasised by the threefold "Woe to you . . ." which unmistakably joins the two chapters together (5:18; 6:1, 4, *RSV*). The first "woe" is addressed to those who foolishly "desire the day of the Lord" through a complete misconception of its character; the second, to those "at ease in Zion"; and the third, to those who "lie upon beds of ivory."

Taking yet another sidelong glance at Judah, Amos links Zion with Samaria in guilt before God (6 : 1). The same tendencies to self-indulgence and moral decadence were manifest in both kingdoms—as represented by their capital cities—albeit they were worse in Israel than in Judah. Having connected the two together in condemnation, Amos again concentrates his message upon Israel. This latter part of the lamentation is largely repetitive, spelling out in detail the crimes of the people, and their consequent penalty.

How astounding it is that those who make their homes near the mouth of a volcano, imagine it to be the safest place in the world! So these besotted Israelites "feel secure in the mountains of Samaria," which seemed at that time so prosperous and peaceful. They little thought, despite the prophet's clear warning, how soon the volcano was to erupt! Their wealth gave them inflated ideas of their own worth and importance; in their own eyes they were "the chief of the nations," whom the rest of the world courted and sought to imitate (6 : 1). With a dramatic gesture Amos invites them to take a look at neighbouring states which had been vanquished: was Israel any better, in any respect, than these had been? They too had acted as if the day of disaster would never come: *but it had*! Let Israel heed the warning (6 : 2–3).

In his third "Woe" oracle the prophet gives a graphic word-picture of the sensuous luxury of the newly-rich—when not lying upon beds ostentatiously decorated with ivory, they sprawled upon couches, indulging the fastidious greediness of the gourmet, drinking bowls of wine, anointing themselves with expensive perfumes—and "not grieving for the affliction of Joseph" (6 : 6). They thought they had everything heart could wish for; but they lacked what was supremely needful—a discernment of the true state of affairs, and a heart to put it right.

"Therefore . . ." (6 : 7). Once again the inevitable sequence, like the sounding of the knell of doom. The richest and most pampered should be the first to go into captivity; and the prophet uses the strongest terms to express the Lord's abhorrence of the manner of life he has described (6 : 8): "I abhor the pride of Jacob, and hate his palaces . . ." His "clean sweep" of this depraved people would leave scarcely a survivor (6 : 9). A kinsman coming to bury the bones of a relative would speak with bated breath, for fear of the anger of the Lord so plainly and devastatingly descended upon His people.

Then in a striking parable-illustration Amos asks, "Do horses plunge over precipices? Or do people plough the sea with oxen?" (6 : 12). But Israel was acting as foolishly as that, by perverting justice and transmuting righteousness into wormwood. Now, through forsaking justice, they would meet judgment. They had gloried in their clever schemings, and in petty victories in capturing two towns, Lo-debar and Karnaim, from the Syrians; but Jehovah's rod of chastisement was ready for use (6 : 14): and its stroke was swiftly to fall upon them.

8

Jehovah's Plumbline

In the closing section of his book, chapters 7–9, Amos records a series of five visions given him, confirming the divine judgment upon Israel. Three of these begin with the phrase, "Thus hath the Lord God showed unto me . . ." (7 : 1, 4; 8 : 1); one with the slightly abbreviated "Thus He showed me . . ." (7 : 7); and finally, "I saw the Lord . . ." (9 : 1).

Three of these five visions are described in chapter 7. The first two are of particular interest, for they reveal a new aspect of the ministry of Amos, that of intercessor for Israel. They also indicate the compassion and forbearance of God, in responding to the pleadings of Amos and moderating the severity of His chastening of Israel—until that solemn hour when the nation's "day of grace" had expired, and irrevocable, unrelieved judgment came upon them.

In a few terse phrases the prophet tells how God "formed grasshoppers"—that is, locusts in the laval stage—early in the season; and these developed into a formidable swarm "after the king's mowing" (7 : 1). The first cutting of grass was evidently claimed by the king as a tax-in-kind, for the sustenance of the royal horses and herds. Afterwards the main mowings would follow. So large a swarm of locusts at such a time would spell complete devastation and disaster. This was possibly the "visitation" referred to in 4 : 9. When they had devoured the grass, however, and before they totally despoiled other crops, Amos appealed to the Lord, "O Lord God, forgive, I beseech Thee: for by whom shall Jacob arise, for he is small" (7 : 2); or, as *RSV* renders the latter part of the verse, "How can Jacob stand? He is so small!"

This may seem a strange plea, at a time when Israel was at the zenith of its prosperity and power. God sees differently from men, however. For, despite all its vaunted greatness and glory, Israel *was* "small," not only in comparison with the great powers, but in the eyes of God and of His prophet. A more sombre interpretation has been suggested, however: that the prophet, by using the name "Jacob," alludes to the small remnant who were the true spiritual descendants of the patriarch. The apostate rich had forfeited that relationship and all that it implied of covenant grace—just as the Jews of a later generation had, who claimed, "Abraham is our father," only to receive our Lord's stinging reply, "If ye were Abraham's children, ye would do the works of Abraham . . . ye are of your father the devil . . ." (John 8 : 39, 44). The poor rural folk, whom the prosperous city-dwellers despised and despoiled, were the true people of God. Crushed and "small" indeed, the plague of locusts would have affected them most disastrously; and so in pity God heard the prayer of Amos on their behalf.

The proud and self-inflated court, the aristocracy and merchants would have squirmed to know that they had been spared hunger and ruin through the prayers of the prophet, and on *this* plea! But so it was: "The Lord repented concerning this: It shall not be, saith the Lord" (7 : 3). Explaining that this is an anthropomorphic expression (see 7 : 6; Gen. 6 : 6; 1 Sam. 15 : 35; Jonah 3 : 9), *Wycliffe* adds, "God did not change His mind, as men do, but changed His course of action, which is consistent with his eternal unchangeableness."

In the second vision (7 : 4–5), the prophet sees "a judgment by fire" (*RSV*) prepared by the Lord. This is a dramatic description of such intense summer heat as would bring about a drought so severe as to exhaust the waters "of the great deep"—the subterranean sources of the springs and rivers—as in the days of Elijah. Once more Amos intercedes, "O Lord God, cease, I beseech Thee": and again the same gracious response is given as before (7 : 6, cf. v. 3). It is moving to read of this compassionate concern of the prophet from Judah for the guilty people to whom he was God's messenger; and to realise that his tenderness was but a reflection of his Lord's. It was the Spirit of God impelling him in this, as in every aspect of his prophetic office. God desired to demonstrate to the prophet, and through his ministry to the nation, His forbearance and loving kindness, His readiness to respond to any appeal from His people.

These two brief oracles re-emphasise the potency of prayer; the part it plays in the outworking of the divine purposes; the fact that God hears and answers the prayers of the few—and even of one faithful servant of His—on behalf of the sinful many.

Ellison, consonant with his theory that these visions preceded the ministry of Amos in Israel, regards these answers to the prophet's intercession as occurring at that time. He identifies these first two visions, as some other commentators do—in the reverse order—with the "beginning of the roll of judgments in 4:6–9." We think it best to consider the entire section, however, in relation to its place in the book.

The third vision (7 : 7–9) has no such happy ending as the first two. The Lord standing by a wall, with plumbline in hand, revealing starkly its out-of-true state, silenced the prophet: in the light of the total failure of the nation to measure up to God's righteous standards, or to respond to His grace, he could only acknowledge that mercy had exhausted its efforts and the time for judgment had come. In solemn condemnation God said, "I will not again pass by them any more." With the spelling-out of the sentence characteristic of this book, Amos records the words of the Lord: "The high places of Isaac shall be desolate, and the sanctuary of Israel shall be laid waste: and I will rise against the house of Jeroboam with the sword."

The repeated use of the names of the patriarchs, Isaac, Jacob and Joseph, in this section of the book, is particularly impressive. It is as if God determinedly recalls the early days of His "espousals" with the children of Israel, the high hopes and "first love" of those days. Alas that their apostasy brought them to this hour of doom: yet His promises to the fathers were never forgotten, and the very use of their names seems a pledge that He will yet fulfil His purposes as promised to them, despite the failings of their descendants. Albeit through a despised "remnant," He would bring to pass all that He had foretold to Abraham and his seed. In the immediate present, however, they could not presume further upon His covenant grace: their sin would be punished, and they would be judged, in the Assyrian assault.

In the rest of the chapter Amos—or the disciples of his who compiled the book which bears his name (if indeed that was the case, as some scholars suggest)—describes an attack upon him by Amaziah, the chief priest at Bethel, and the prophet's rejoinder (7: 10–17). First Amaziah sent an exasperated message to the king, alleging that Amos had "conspired against" him by foretelling the conquest and captivity of Israel. In truth, the prophet's condemnation of the national evils in general, and the unrighteousness of the rich in particular, might have been regarded as inciting an uprising on the part of the poor of the land. Small wonder that Amaziah protested, "The land is not able to bear all his words!"

Jeroboam seems to have disregarded the priest's expostulation. He either dismissed the admonitions of Amos as harmless hot air, or knew the people to be too dispirited to rise up in rebellion. As for the warnings of invasion, they were the ravings of a fanatic! The priest could deal with a recalcitrant, half-crazed prophet! This attitude of the king exemplifies the opinion he held of the "prophets" of the northern cult and sanctuary; he not unnaturally regarded Amos, whom he knew only by report, as being in the same category.

Unsupported by the king, therefore, Amaziah himself turned upon Amos and angrily demanded that he should "flee away into the land of Judah, and there eat bread, and prophesy there: but prophesy not again any more in Bethel, for it is the king's sanctuary, and it is a temple of the kingdom" (7 : 12–13). In the idiom of today, this might be paraphrased: "Get out of our country, and back into your own! Take your miserable prophesyings to your own people: they might need them; we don't! Perhaps you can persuade them to believe you—and pay you for haranguing them! Don't darken again *these* doors of the king's sanctuary and the centre of our nation's religious life. We can manage our own affairs without your help, thank you!"

In dignified yet pungent reply, Amos declared, in familiar words, "I was no prophet, neither was I a prophet's son; but . . . the Lord took me as I followed the flock, and said unto me, Go, prophesy unto my people Israel . . ." (7 : 14–15). He was not denying his prophetic office, but declaring bluntly that he was no professional "prophetic practitioner." He had not passed through any "school for prophets," nor did he aspire to any position of prestige or authority. He wanted no patronage or payment. Indeed, he indignantly repudiated the suggestion that he was seeking personal profit: he had no need of it, for he had his own means of livelihood. Further, he had no axe to grind; no ambition to fulfil, nor anything to gain by bringing Israel the word of the Lord. He was there by divine compulsion, and that alone. While pursuing his chosen avocation God had called and commissioned him to be His messenger to Israel. It was a condemnation of Amaziah and all the cultic priests and prophets of the kingdom, that God could use none of them to proclaim His word, but had to send a layman from Judah.

For Amaziah's betrayal of his priestly office; for his guilty part in not only condoning Israel's apostasy and idolatry, but leadership in it, stern judgment would come upon him and his family. For commanding the prophet of God not to prophesy in Bethel, he should hear a prophecy addressed to himself—that his wife should be violated by the invaders, and his sons and daughters slain; that he should see the land over-run and ravaged, and then should be carried away into captivity, to die "in a polluted (*i.e.*, heathen) land." He should learn through bitter experience that Amos was indeed a prophet of the Lord, by the fulfilment of this word; he should see also the coming to pass of the other prophesies he had tried to quench. Too late he would recognise that Amos indeed spoke the word of the Lord.

9

Fruit—and Famine

A basket of summer fruit. Could any phrase be evocative of more pleasant sensations, or conjure up a more agreeable mental picture, than this? The sight and smell of fruit are delightsome to practically everybody; a basket of varied fruits is not only pleasing to the eye, but appealing to the taste of all. Alas, the phrase at the beginning of the fourth of the five visions of Amos, "Thus hath the Lord God shewed unto me: and behold a basket of summer fruit" (8:1) is, in our English translations, misleading. No such happy connotation is imparted to the phrase by the prophet. On the contrary, the words "summer fruit" convey the thought, says Howard, of "over-ripe, and about to decay," a rendering supported by other scholars.

How bitterly disappointing it would be, to anticipate the enjoyment of luscious-looking fruit, only to find it rotten right through. This is the picture given here of Jehovah's disappointment in His people.

The significance of this metaphor is stark and sombre: the basket of fruit indicated that the "summer" of divine forbearance and blessing was ended: winter with its icy winds was imminent for Israel. Harvest time had come, but its fruits were corrupt. Throughout Scripture, harvest is related to spiritual fruition in the life of individuals and of the nation; and to divine judgment upon their failure to produce "fruit unto righteousness." Well might these people say, with those of Judah in Jeremiah's day, "The harvest is past, the summer is ended, and we are not saved" (Jer. 8:20).

Once again spelling out in detail the judgment that was soon to break upon them, Amos proceeded, "Then said the Lord upto me, The end is come upon my people Israel: I will not again pass by them any more" (8:2). Some commentators think that we have here a play upon words, since in the Hebrew "ripe fruit" (*qayis*) and "end" (*qes*) are very similar. Its own condition of spiritual and moral decay had brought upon the nation its doom. Their evil manner of life was ripe for judgment. And lest anyone should even now be in doubt what that would imply, Amos declared, "The songs of the temple shall be howlings in that day, saith the Lord God: there shall be many dead bodies in every place; they shall cast them forth with silence" (8:3). It is a solemnising picture of devastating national disaster, involving the complete overthrow of their idolatrous shrine, and the carnage of conquest on every hand. Moreover, the prophet made clear that this should be no localised or limited subjugation by Assyria: it should engulf "every place," and the terror of it should benumb the senses, subduing the very cries of grief of the bereaved "remnant" remaining in the land.

Again the prophet repeats the reason for such unmitigated penalty: their utter disregard of moral and ethical standards; the rapacity of the rich, and their relentless oppression of the poor, had sealed their fate. "Hear this," Amos exhorted them, "you who trample upon the needy, and bring the poor of the land to an end . . ." (8:4). So eager for gain were they; so obsessed with the fever of money-making, that they were impatient of the restraints imposed upon their trading by observance of the Sabbath and festive days, and had thought only for their bargainings: "saying, when will the new moon be over, that we may sell grain? And the Sabbath, that we may offer wheat for sale, that we may make the ephah small and the shekel great, and deal deceitfully with false balances . . ." (8 : 5). Sharp practice of every kind was indulged, in this greed for gain, from cheating with scales to fiddling with money.

How unchanged is human nature! These self-same sins of fraud and deception, falsehood and duplicity still characterise much that goes on under the name of business. This is ever the cancer at the heart of materialism; that which makes so much modern money-making, also, rotten at the core.

This fever to get-rich-quickly rendered these Israelite tycoons regardless of human considerations: anything or anybody could be exploited to serve their ends. They even schemed to "buy the poor for silver, and the needy for a pair of sandals." By distraining their property for debts, they compelled the farmers and small-holders to sell themselves into slavery for a mere pittance—as Amos so graphically says, for the price of a pair of shoes. So devious were they, that they actually tried to sell husks in place of grain! (8 : 6): which is not so improbable as it sounds, in the light of some present-day business scandals.

All this was observed by God, who "hath sworn by the excellency of Jacob, surely I will never forget any of their works" (8:7). This most solemn adjuration attests the certainty of judgment. With striking metaphor, Amos likens the overwhelming assault of the Assyrians to "the flood of Egypt," the overflowing of its banks by the Nile, submerging the entire countryside. Even so should Israel be "tossed about and drowned" (8:8).

Then follows a passage about which the scholars speculate and dispute: "And it shall come to pass in that day, saith the Lord God, that I will cause the sun to go down at noon, and I will darken the earth in the clear day" (8:9). Can this be related to recorded events occurring at this time, such as the eclipse of the sun in 763 BC, or is it highly symbolic language descriptive of the terrors of the judgment to come upon them? Or again, is it apocalyptic, alluding to the final judgment? We must leave that argument to others; and they will probably never resolve it! Certainly no ordinary catastrophe is envisaged here: whoever might be the human instruments engaged therein, the one bringing *this* sequence of events to pass was God himself: Adonai Jehovah, the Lord their God. In the hour of His ultimate judgments no way or place of alleviation can be found; and against them there can be no appeal. It will indeed be a "bitter day" (8:10).

In that awesome hour the stricken people will realise, too late, the value of that which they most wantonly neglected: they will hunger and thirst, not for food and drink, but for the word of God, the bread and water of life. Alas, they will cry out in vain then for that which they formerly spurned; for "I will send a famine in the land, not a famine of bread, nor a thirst for water, but of hearing the words of the Lord." The ministry of the prophets, long unheeded, will be longed for unavailingly: their message will have found its sad fulfilment.

So will it be at the end of the age, when this day of grace gives place to the final judgment. In vain will men seek the mercy of God when its age-long appeal to them is terminated; the word of divine compassion, when its work is done. The Gospel has a stern note, which will take over entirely from its winsome call for repentance and faith: the wrath of the Lamb will come upon all who have rejected His redeeming grace. "They shall wander," as did the stricken Israelites, "from sea to sea, and from the north even to the east, they shall run to and fro to seek the word of the Lord, and shall not find it" (8:12).

A particularly poignant note sounds forth here, as Amos proceeds, "In that day shall the fair virgins and young men faint for thirst" (8:13). The young will suffer most, as they do in every disaster brought about by their elders: for this calamity will come upon them through the sin of their seniors, rather than their own. It is the responsibility of each generation to teach and train its children in the word and ways of the Lord. No richer heritage can be imparted to young people than the influences of a godly home. On the other hand, an evil and perverse generation reproduces its evils in magnified form in its offspring. That tragedy of Israel in the times of Amos is ours today.

The concluding word, however, foretells the total destruction of idolatry and idolaters in Israel. "Those who swear by Ashimar of Samaria, and say, As thy god lives, O Dan, and, As the way of Beer-sheba lives, they shall fall . . ." (8:14). All who participated in the cult worship of Israel, or trusted in the gods of other nations, should perish: and there is a fearsome finality in the concluding phrase, ". . . and never rise up again." No "Gospel of the second chance" here, or elsewhere in the Scriptures. Rather, the Word of God consistently makes plain that, as men sow, they reap; as they react to the revealed will of God, they determine their eternal destiny. As in the days of the patriarchs and of the prophets, so in these sophisticated times: "Be not deceived; God is not mocked: for whatsoever a man soweth, that shall he also reap. For he that soweth to his flesh shall of the flesh reap corruption; but he that soweth to the Spirit shall of the Spirit reap life everlasting" (Gal. 6:7–8).

10

Doom—and New Dawn

Two key-notes have sounded throughout the prophecies of Amos: that the judgment about to come upon Israel was occasioned by the apostasy of the nation from the Lord their God, and by the oppression of the poorer members of the community by the ruling and prosperous minority. Ungodliness and social unrighteousness often go hand-in-hand: not invariably, for—to look no further afield than Britain—a good deal of the latter prevailed when religion flourished. But true godliness could not remain oblivious of the evils of this situation, and social reform sprang from the most spiritually-minded among the privileged classes. It is correct to say, therefore, despite the contradictory evidence of social history, that ungodliness is the root cause of social evils, especially the exploitation of the poor by the rich. God is grieved by both the root and the fruit; and His condemnation of them runs like a refrain through the entire Scriptures. Those people who speak and act as if God were concerned only with people's religious beliefs and practices—their Sunday-best profession and behaviour—and not with their work-a-day lives and activities, can never intelligently have read their Bibles. God hates injustice, as He hates idolatry. His stern indignation against heartless tyrants sounds throughout this book of Amos, as in other prophets. Nevertheless, while judgment is pronounced on Israel on this score, the final word relates to the greatest, most grievous sin: the source from which all others proceed—departure from God, defiance of His law, and disregard of His will.

The final oracle of Amos, in chapter 9, therefore strikes at the heart of Israel's apostate condition—its degraded cult worship, still in the name of Jehovah, but in fact violating His most explicit commands, desecrating His holy name, and substituting all the evil accompaniments of idolatry for the worship of the living God in spirit and in truth. It was at the shrine of Bethel, "the king's sanctuary" as Amaziah the priest had called it (7:13) that the prophet "saw the Lord standing upon (or 'beside,' *RSV*) the altar"

(9:1). Nowhere else in the Bible is such a phrase to be found. This last of the five visions of Amos differs from the previous four, in that God Himself appeared; and Amos saw Him, not "high and lifted up," as did Isaiah afterwards in the temple at Jerusalem, but standing at the altar to execute the judgment already pronounced. There is striking symbolism in the phrase. The altar was the place of sacrifice; of approach to God in repentance and in worship: the place where God met with His covenant people. By their evil attitudes and practices, however, they had desecrated the altar, and revealed their disregard for all that it truly symbolised and expressed: and so God now meets with them there, not in grace but in judgment.

Judgment, said Peter, centuries later, must begin at the house of God; and that is true not only of the New Testament times: the apostle was enunciating a consistent principle of the divine dealings with men. So the first word of the Lord from the altar is, "Smite the capitals until the thresholds shake, and shatter them on the heads of all the people . . ." (*RSV*). Smiting the lintel (*AV*), or chapiters (*RV*), would ensure the collapse of the whole building, and destroy its priests and worshippers—who probably fled in panic to the sanctuary when Assyria launched its *blitzkrieg* against Israel, and in doing so all unwittingly executed the judgment of God. "And what are left of them," the Lord adds, "I will slay with the sword."

In the language of prophetic hyperbole, Amos proceeds, "Though they dig into Sheol, from there shall my hand take them; though they climb up to heaven from there will I bring them down . . ." (9:2–3). Such severe words from the lips of the Father of mercies and God of love, fill the heart with awe as we read them; and it is with bated breath that we proceed, "Though they go into captivity before their enemies, there will I command the sword, and it shall slay them; and I will set my eyes upon them for evil and not for good" (9:4).

Then in a passage of exquisite beauty, Amos magnifies the One who thus brings His righteous judgments to pass in the earth—

> The Lord, God of hosts,
> He who touches the earth and it melts,
>   and who dwell in it mourn,
> and all of it rises like the Nile,
>   and sinks again, like the Nile of Egypt;

who builds His upper chambers in the heavens,
and founds His vault upon the earth;
who calls for the waters of the sea,
and pours them out upon the surface of the earth—
the Lord is His name.

This paean of praise; this awed adoration of the prophet, expresses his personal response to the fearsome pronouncement he had heard from the lips of God at Bethel's altar, and in turn passed on to the people of Israel. It is God Himself who is to bring upon His chosen race this consequence of their guilt; who is to overwhelm them in the Assyrian invasion as irresistibly and totally as the Nile overflows its adjacent countryside. The Lord of heaven and earth is on the march against them!

Then in anguished repetition of the reasons for His dealing thus with them, God says, "Are you not like the Ethiopians to me, O people of Israel?" (9 : 7). Israel were His covenant people, His chosen; but He was not untrue to His covenant when dealing with them in judgment. Rather, they had forfeited the benefits of the covenant by their unfaithfulness to it: indeed, thereby they had become "like the Ethiopians to me." It is perhaps needless to remark, as one commentator does, that there is no suggestion of colour prejudice in this comment: the Ethiopians are mentioned only because they were the most far-off people known to the Israelites of those days: the most remote strangers and foreigners. Thus graphically Amos illustrates Israel's alienation from God.

In assertion of their special relationship to God, Israel delighted to boast that He had brought them out of Egypt, and into the promised land. But equally He had brought the Philistines from Caphtor, and the Syrians from Kir! (9 : 7). He is the sovereign Lord of all nations, and will judge them all in righteousness, Israel included.

Behold, the eyes of the Lord God are upon the sinful kingdom,
and I will destroy it from the surface of the ground;
except that I will not utterly destroy the house of Jacob,
says the Lord.

His people had become so sinful that, like the Amorites whom they displaced, the cup of their iniquity was full; therefore a like calamity should fall upon them as they had executed upon those earlier sinners. God has no favourites. He does not wink at sin in those He has greatly blessed, any more than in the most rebellious. Israel should perish, as did the original inhabitants of the land.

In the operation of His judgments, however, the declared purpose of God should be fulfilled, for even in the overwhelming of Israel and their scattering among all nations, He would sift them as wheat: the sinners among His people should die by the sword, "yet shall not the least grain (*AV*, 'pebble,' *RSV*) fall upon the earth" (9:9). A residue of the righteous should be preserved, through whom, pitiable though they might seem to be, the promises of God should be fulfilled.

It is arresting that the very last phrase in this final oracle of Amos at Bethel is a repudiation by the people of belief in his message: they declared "The evil shall not overtake or meet us" (9:10). How blind they were; how besotted! How deaf their ears to the truth; to the most solemn warnings from Almighty God, through His prophet. No such dreadful calamity as he described could happen to *them*! This was mere alarmist talk; sheer scaremongering!

That is how they reacted then; and today the majority of people react in precisely the same way to the messenger of God who, like the prophet of old, has the courage to give warning of wrath to come. But that message will have the same eventual vindication as did that of Amos.

His ministry in Bethel completed, the herdman of Tekoa added to his record—perhaps after he returned home—an epilogue, so contrasting in tenor to the book as a whole that critics consider it to be by another hand, and probably post-exilic. Conservative scholars affirm, however, that internal evidence for the authenticity of 9:11–15 as an integral part of the book is convincing. It is certainly in keeping with the practice of the prophets generally, even after a ministry of stern condemnation, to look forward to the final realisation of the revealed will of God. So Amos declares, in the name of the Lord, "In that day I will raise up the booth of David that is fallen, and repair its breaches . . ." This is not a sentimental "happy ending" to a sombre story; rather is it the strong assertion of the undeviating loyalty of God to His pledged word, and unfaltering pursuit of His predicted purposes. The promises to the fathers, explicitly confirmed to David, are to be fully realised in the person of David's greater Son. The kingdom rent asunder by Israel's rejection of the house of David, should be reunited in the reign of his Messiah-Son. "The tabernacle of David," says

Matthew Henry, "means his house and family"—and other commentators agree. James, the brother of Jesus, as chairman of the council in Jerusalem (Acts 15) quoted this verse as signifying the formation of a new community of the people of God; the new-covenant Israel, comprised of both Jews and Gentiles.

We have, in these concluding glowing words of Amos a prophetic preview of the millennial kingdom, when "the plowman shall overtake the reaper, and the treader of grapes him who sows the seed"—a favourite text for Harvest Festivals, taken alas, all too often, right out of its context. The bounty of God in nature is often depicted in Scripture as an evidence of His sovereign grace and fatherly beneficence, and here it reaches the highest peak of abundance. The Israel of God shall then be united and complete; eternal security will banish every fear, and the joy of the Lord shall be their perpetual experience. What a prospect for the redeemed!

III

HOSEA

PORTRAYAL AND PROPHECY

HOSEA: LAST PROPHET TO ISRAEL

Hosea has many claims to distinction. He was the first, and only, prophet of Israel whose oracles were recorded in writing. And he was the last to bring the word of the Lord to the northern kingdom, before its overthrow. Moreover, he was the most "human" and tender of God's messengers to His apostate people. A younger contemporary of Amos, Hosea gives no indication in his book whether or not he heard that "southerner" declare the word of the Lord at Bethel. In any event, he would know about him and his startling pronouncements. Whereas Amos prophesied in the prosperous and peaceful days of Jeroboam II, Hosea witnessed the confusion which followed the death of that king—with internal dynastic strife, and the increasingly aggressive activities of Assyria threatening the very existence of Israel—prophesying, apparently, until the very eve of the catastrophic assault upon Samaria. Israel, in this uneasy and ominous era, behaved like a "silly dove," seeking alternately alliance with Egypt and with Assyria. In this deteriorating situation, presaging final doom, Hosea portrayed and prophesied the word of the Lord.

I

Preparation of a Prophet

HOSEA had the sad distinction of being God's last prophetic voice to Israel, the doomed northern kingdom which had, from the days of the mighty Elijah, and his equally eminent successor Elisha, paid but scant attention even to such outstanding spokesmen from God. Amos had but recently fulfilled his brief prophetic ministry at Bethel, and had been ignominiously rebuffed and repudiated by Amaziah the priest. God's judgment upon the apostate nation had been pronounced by the "herdman of Tekoa," and it fell to the lot of Hosea to utter the Lord's final word—a word of mingled warning, appeal, and confirmation of the condemnation already declared. Perhaps no book of the Bible reveals more clearly than this of Hosea, the travail of God over His wayward people.

More than any other prophet, Hosea portrayed in his personal and domestic experience the message he was inspired to deliver. Other prophets sometimes *enacted* their messages, as when Isaiah dressed as a slave, or Jeremiah wore a yoke. Hosea, however, was much more intimately identified with the message he bore; for the tragedy of his broken family life, through the unfaithfulness of his wife, Gomer, not only portrayed the unfaithfulness of Israel to God, but gave him a keen and compassionate understanding of what the nation's spiritual adultery meant to the Lord. Indeed, his prophetic ministry was born out of the travail of his own marital sorrow; his experience opened his eyes to the national situation, and gave him both the burden of his message and the compassionate manner of its delivery. No prophet sounded more profound depths of anguish in proclaiming the warning of impending judgment than Hosea; none pleaded with an apostate people more poignantly.

The book of Hosea is in two parts—his personal story in chapters 1–3; and his prophetic utterances, 4–14. The two sections are quite separate; there is no mention in the autobiographical chapters of the public ministry, nor any allusion in the prophecies to Hosea's exemplification of the utterances he made. The first part explains and underlies the prophetic ministry; yet when fulfilling that ministry Hosea did not draw attention to himself, but proclaimed the word of the Lord. We are able to see the relationship between the man and his message more clearly, probably, than his contemporaries did. This story is told, most emphatically, for *our* learning, as much as for his own day and generation.

The development of Hosea's prophetic ministry from his personal sorrow gives us a graphic, and indeed unique, glimpse-behind-the-scenes into the divine method of preparation of a man for public proclamation of God's word. It is a mystery which has probably intrigued every reader of the Bible—exactly *how* the word of God came to the inspired prophets.

We are given some idea how certain of the prophets were prepared through long years—such as Moses, in the court of Pharaoh and then in the pasture-lands of Moab; Samuel, in the tabernacle at Shiloh from childhood; and Elisha, disciple and successor of the great Elijah. Isaiah gives us an account of his commissioning, in a vision of the divine glory granted to him in the temple, which never fails to awe and thrill us as we read it long centuries afterward. Elijah, on the other hand, first appears on the scene fully-fledged, dramatically confronting Ahab with the ringing words, "As the Lord God of Israel liveth, before whom I stand, there shall not be dew nor rain these years, but according to my word . . ."

None of these stories, however, answers our questions regarding the method of communication of the word of the Lord *to* the prophet, that he might give it forth. It is true, God spoke initially to the young Samuel in audible voice, so that he thought it was the aged Eli calling him. We cannot conceive, however, that God continued thus to reveal His mind and purposes to Samuel, and that all his prophetic utterances were merely a repeating of what he had heard in audible communications from God. We are thrown back upon the declaration of Peter, that "holy men of God spake as they were moved by the Holy Ghost" (2 Pet. 1 : 21).

In Hosea, however, we have clearer indication than in any other instance, of how that experience of being "moved by the Holy Ghost" came about. The word of God came *to* him, as a personal constraint and command, before it was transmuted into a commissioning for public ministry. Hosea is careful to emphasise this, for in chapter 1 the affirmation, "The word of the Lord that came *unto Hosea*" (v. 1) is followed by the insistence that the Lord said *to Hosea* (v. 2), and the Lord said *unto him* (vv. 4, 6, 9).

Now Hosea is by no means alone in stressing that the word of the Lord came to him in a personal capacity, before he gave it forth publicly. The same claim is made by Joel, Jonah, Micah, Zephaniah and Zechariah (1 : 1, in each case). Others state that the word, or vision, or "burden" was given them, concerning those to whom they prophesied—Ezekiel 1 : 1; Amos 1 : 1; Obadiah 1 : 1; Nahum 1 : 1; Habakkuk 1 : 1; Haggai 1 : 1; and Malachi 1 : 1. In all these cases, however, the prophets go on immediately to proclaim publicly what had been committed to them. Only in the story of Hosea are we given an unfolding of the process by which the word *to* the prophet became the word *through* him.

Here is a Scriptural principle of the first importance, however: that only those who themselves hear, receive, trust and obey the word of God are truly qualified to declare it. Not all who assumed the rôle of prophet in Israel were thus qualified; nor are all who purport to speak in the name of God today, entitled to fulfil that office. There were false prophets then; and they are equally numerous now. There were men who, through heredity or training or patronage, had come to be accepted as prophets although lacking every evidence of godliness and spiritual grace (cf. 1 Kings 22 : 11–25; Jer. 23 : 25). There were even high priests who harried the Lord of glory to a shameful death on a cross.

No other qualification can make a man a prophet of the Lord, than that the word of the Lord has come *to him*. That is the essential *sine qua non*. Every true preacher of the Gospel speaks out of a profound personal experience of the communication of the word of God to his own heart and life; he needs must have heard the voice of God before he attempts to stand before others as a messenger of God. A mere knowledge of the Bible is not enough; it is the word of God *come alive*, spoken by the Spirit to the individual as a communication of God to him, that inspires prophetic witness. It would simplify a good many controversies and current problems if we were to recognise this fact.

On the other hand, not every man to whom the word of the Lord comes is necessarily a prophet: the Lord is not so niggardly in communication of His word as that! To every born-again believer, God draws near and speaks, by His Spirit, through the Scriptures. It is thus that the Bible becomes a lamp unto our feet and a light unto our path; God's word *to us*, to enlighten, guide and strengthen in Christian discipleship. We have erred, perhaps, as much in urging some such to preach, as in listening to others who lack this essential qualification.

To Hosea, the word of God came first as a simple command—to marry; and in the experiences which followed he was led, ever more deeply, into an understanding of the mind and heart of the Lord, and also of the behaviour of His people, Israel. This two-fold realisation—or rather, revelation, by the word of the Lord—became the impetus of his prophetic ministry. He saw the conduct of the people of God, and its consequences, from the standpoint of the Almighty: and he could not but speak what he had seen and heard. That had been his preparation as a prophet.

2

Adultery: Physical and Spiritual

NOTHING is known about Hosea apart from the self-portrait he gives us in his book. He lived in the northern kingdom of Israel, in the era immediately preceding its overthrow —probably witnessing the carrying away of its people into captivity by Assyria, although he makes no actual mention of that. While Hosea was fulfilling his ministry in the north, his great contemporary, Isaiah, was prophesying in the southern kingdom of Judah.

The majority of his prophecies were addressed to Israel, with occasional sidelong references to Judah—as in 1:7. Incidentally, it is perhaps because of his realisation, through the prophecies he was inspired to utter, that Judah was to be the means of the ultimate fulfilment of the purposes of God for His people, that Hosea dates his book (1:1) primarily by the kings of Judah and only secondarily by Jeroboam II of Israel. He recognised in Judah the permanent element in the continuing history of the covenant race.

His warning of impending judgment upon Israel fell on heedless ears, for the most part; for calamity never seemed more unlikely than in the reign of Jeroboam. An unusually prolonged period of peace and prosperity had fostered a false sense of security, which in turn encouraged self-indulgence, apostasy, and lowering of moral standards. To this spiritually adulterous generation Hosea sounded out the notes of final admonition and entreaty, in the Name of the Lord—alas, in vain.

Before he could diagnose the nation's *malaise*, however, and tell forth the word of the Lord concerning it, Hosea had to apprehend the full significance and sorrow of it through personal experience. His domestic tragedy became the means of revelation from God of the true state of affairs between Himself and His people, Israel. Unfaithful Gomer became to Hosea the personification and exemplification of the adulterous "wife" of Jehovah; and amid his own distress he was even more concerned for the sorrow of God and the fate of the nation. Indeed, as this situation was progressively understood by Hosea, it becomes difficult to distinguish, in his narrative, between his personal story and its parabolic application to the nation. The two intermingle and intertwine; as when Paul, writing to the Ephesians about husband-and-wife relationships, speaks also concerning Christ and the church—and we can hardly tell which remarks apply to the earthly, and which to the heavenly relationship! They are, of course, true of both. Likewise Hosea writes of Gomer and Israel; his anguished experience, and God's.

The unfaithfulness of the covenant people of God is repeatedly likened, in Scripture, to adultery (Jer. 3 : 9; Ezek. 16 : 30–32; 23 : 37). Israel was His "bride" (Isa. 62 : 5; Jer. 2 : 32; 33 : 11); a "virgin" chosen from among the nations (Jer. 14 : 17; 18 : 13; 31 : 4, 21; Lam. 1 : 15; 2 : 13; Joel 1 : 8; Amos 5 : 2). This husband-wife relationship should have been Israel's chief joy and profoundest satisfaction. Instead, they consistently violated the vows upon which the covenant was based, and turned aside to false gods—Baalim, and the idols of the nations they inwardly despised.

All this was shown to Hosea through the distress of his own marital tragedy. By whatever means the word of the Lord might have come to other prophets, it was needful that Hosea, before he could fulfil his distinctive ministry, should enter into the full poignancy of the situation through personal domestic travail. A further divine purpose also is clear: many people who would not pay attention to what he might say, nevertheless observed his life. He learned the vital importance of *living out* the word of God; he anticipated the demand of Paul, that the people of God should be "living epistles" for Him.

In order, therefore, not only to understand but also to portray, in enacted parable, the unfaithfulness of Israel to God, Hosea was commanded to "take . . . a wife of whoredoms" (1 : 2). This verse poses one of the great moral problems of Scripture. How, it is asked, could a holy God command a man like Hosea to marry a harlot?

Such questions cannot be burked; and it must be confessed that Bible students have held differing views on the matter. It is important to remember, however, that Hosea is telling the story after the events happened—as an historian might; and it is generally agreed that the disputed phrase describes Gomer as she *proved herself to be,* and not her condition when Hosea wooed her. God commanded him to take Gomer as his wife, and she became an adulteress; in that sense, God required him to "take . . . a wife of whoredoms."

Not only would it be incompatible with the character of God to direct the prophet to marry a woman who was already a harlot, but this would violate the parallel which their marriage was to present, with the relationship between God and His people—for Israel was not spiritually a "harlot" when God betrothed her to Himself, but became one afterward. True, God foreknew Israel's apostasy, even when He "betrothed" her; likewise Gomer, although a pure virgin, was a potential adulteress, who in unfaithfulness to Hosea exemplified the spiritual state of Israel in relation to God.

The drama unfolded slowly, with Hosea gradually realising his wife's true character. This is indicated in the names he gave to the children of the marriage. Strikingly enough, however, he was commanded by God to give them names relative to the national situation rather than his family life—though the personal aspect is reflected therein. His firstborn was therefore called *Jezreel*, a reminder of the blood-guiltiness of Jehu, and a warning of judgment upon Israel. It was also a veiled intimation to Gomer that her guilt was not unobserved and would not be unrebuked. God never condones nor winks at sin, no matter how much it may seem that He does. His longsuffering, and slowness to wrath, are often mistaken for an incapacity to judge; but all who presume upon this will learn their tragic error.

Jezreel occupies a significant place in Israel's history—and especially in relation to the royal house of Ahab. Here, that ignoble king and his even more sinister wife, Jezebel, plotted the death of Naboth and the seizure of his vineyard (1 Kings 21:1–26); here also judgment upon his descendant Joram was executed by the hand of Jehu (2 Kings 9:4–10, 14–26); but although an instrument of divine judgment, Jehu himself displayed so evil a motive and manner that he, in his turn, became the object of judgment (Hosea 1:4–5). More than once in the Old Testament we find this principle enunciated: that those used to bring about the purposes of God will themselves be judged by the same standards as were their victims (Gen. 15:14; Isa. 10:5, 24–27).

Because God is holy and righteous, He is of necessity a God of judgment; but ever in Scripture He is depicted supremely as a God of grace and mercy. Judgment is His "strange work," His "strange act" (Isa. 28:21), necessitated by His character and man's sin. It is, however, never His last word or final act: the entire Scriptures declare that His purposes of grace ultimately triumph over sin and its consequences.

That principle is declared here: this name, Jezreel, not only epitomises the judgment of God upon Israel and its king, but also the eventual prevailing of the divine purposes despite all the failure of men and all the wiles of the evil one—envisaged in verses 10 and 11, Hosea's vision of the redeemed people of God, when "great shall be *the day of Jezreel*." This promise is re-echoed in 2:20–23, when the restored nation will be given this very name: ". . . . I will even betroth thee unto me in righteousness . . . and the earth shall hear Jezreel." It is as if the very memory of past judgment is blotted out; the sting is extracted from the name, so that the people who trembled at the sound of it now rejoice to be called by it. The faithfulness of God to His covenant must finally be vindicated before all heaven and earth, even through judgment, to His glory and His people's eternal good.

Returning to the family history of Hosea, a daughter was born and named *Lo-ruhamah*, "unpitied," intimating a withdrawal of the mercy of God from an unfaithful people—and that an unworthy wife should experience the consequences of her disloyalty. A second son, *Lo-ammi*, "not my people," pronounced God's disavowal of a nation which had forfeited the covenant relationship with which He had blessed them—and indicated the now open breach between husband and wife.

That is a cold summary of Hosea's progressive realisation of Gomer's true character and treacherous conduct, and its portrayal of Israel's harlotry toward God; but there is nothing cold in the prophet's telling of it. His words are suffused with anguish, and tempest-tossed by surging emotions of constant though betrayed love; of alternating hope and despair of her repentance and restoration. Hosea's love did not falter toward adulterous Gomer, much as he grieved over her unfaithfulness; nor does God's toward His apostate people. Hosea was given, by grace from on high, an old-covenant anticipation of the new-covenant revelation of the character of God as love; and he exemplified Paul's inspired declaration that "love never faileth."

3

Children of Whoredom

Unquestionably those born and reared in godly homes have inestimable advantage. How often, at valedictory meetings for missionary recruits, do we hear testimony to the fact that a Christian upbringing has been the supreme earthly factor in their conversion and call to the mission field. In our churches, the great majority of stalwarts who set the tone and bear the burdens are members of families with a tradition for sacrificial Christian service.

On the other hand, we are well aware of the utter lack of God-consciousness—any sense of the reality of things unseen and eternal—which seems to characterise the offspring of godless parents. It is true that this, like every generalisation, is often confounded by the exceptions: many children of devoted Christian parents grow up regardless of religion, while equally many who had no godly influence or example in their homes, come into the reality of true relationship to God in Christ. One of the most heartening features of evangelistic witness today is the high percentage of such young people among those responding to the call for commitment to Christ as Saviour and Lord.

All this does not deeply affect the general pattern, however, that those enjoying the advantages of a godly home become themselves men and women of God in far larger numbers, proportionately, than those lacking such early influence and privilege. Does this mean, then, that the first category are a "favoured race" in comparison with the second?

This problem is age-long. It was voiced in Israel three thousand years ago by those who said, "The fathers have eaten sour grapes, and the children's teeth are set on edge"—for both Jeremiah and Ezekiel quote this as a familiar proverb (Jer. 31 : 29; Ezek. 18 : 2), and both give the same reply: that the assertion is not valid, for God does not deal with individuals according to their heredity or upbringing—"As I live, saith the Lord God, ye shall not have occasion any more to use this proverb in Israel. Behold, all souls are mine; as the soul of the father, so also the soul of the son is mine: the soul that sinneth, it shall die" (Ezek. 18 : 3–4).

Responsibility for attitude toward God, and relationship with Him, is placed squarely upon the shoulders of each individual. God has endowed mankind with the priceless gift of freewill: that gift brings with it inescapable obligation to choose whether or not to trust and obey the word of the Lord—or, in terms of the new covenant, to respond to the Gospel of the grace of God in Christ our Redeemer and Lord. Neglect of the issue is never regarded in Scripture as neutrality: it is, in fact, tantamount to positive rejection. The writer to the Hebrews states this in plainest terms—"How shall we escape if we neglect so great salvation?" (Heb. 2 : 3).

This principle is assumed, rather than explicitly stated, in Hosea 2. How human and how poignant a story it is! The prophet exhorts his children to address one another, not by the names which indicated the consequences of sin—*Lo-ammi*, "Not my people," and *Lo-ruhamah*, "Not pitied"—but rather, by dropping the prefix "*Lo*," to claim the covenant relationship and to call upon the divine grace. "Say ye unto your brethren, *Ammi*; and to your sisters *Ruhamah*." Thus the terror of the names given to them will be neutralised, the sting extracted—just as in the case of Jezreel.

The Lord our God is ever ready to hear the cry of the penitent, and to respond to the least gesture of faith and love toward Him. Grace can prevail over every handicap of birth and bias, of temperament and training. All that God requires is that exercise of choice, that expression of faith, which is invited in the words, "*Say ye . . .*" The voicing of the names *Ammi* and *Ruhamah* would itself establish the relationship which they declare.

"I am the Lord's!" O joy beyond expression,
O sweet response to voice of love divine;
Faith's joyous "Yes" to the assuring whisper,
"Fear not! I have redeemed thee, thou are mine."

The prophet then calls upon his children to plead with their mother (2 : 2), who had separated herself from him and gone after her "lovers" (2 : 5), to abandon her wanton ways. With this appeal he repeats the warning that persistence in adultery will inevitably bring retribution (2:3). Then Hosea reminds the children again that, inheriting their mother's disposition and proclivities, they also will come under judgment if they pursue evil ways (2:4).

Ellison, however, strongly challenges this traditional interpretation of the passage. He says, in *The Prophets of Israel,* "The ambiguity of *Plead with your mother, plead* (cf. Jer. 2:9. *RV*), retained even in *RSV*, is bound to lead to the popular interpretation that Gomer's abandoned babies are to plead with her to return. But like most other sentimental interpretations of Scripture, it is impossible. We must render, *Bring your charge against your mother, bring your charge! For she is not my wife, and I am not her husband.* Israel's one hope is that her own sons should stand up in accusation against her as Ezekiel was later to do with Judah (cf. chs. 16, 20, 23), rebuking her not for her faults but for her fundamental unfaithfulness" (p. 106).

The prophet goes on to expose the blindness and folly of unfaithfulness; for in pursuing "lovers" the faithless wife is forsaking the one who had been bountiful and gracious (2:5). In her avarice she thinks she will gain; that her lovers will give her more than her husband has done—Baal, more than Jehovah. Her adulterous "love" is essentially selfish. And much that parades under the name of love today, as then, is in fact greedy self-love, utterly self-centred and self-seeking—"I will go after my lovers, that give me my bread and my water, my wool and my flax, mine oil and my drink . . ." (2 : 5).

But calculating as it is, self-love greatly errs. This was profoundly true of Israel, as, on a smaller scale, it was of Gomer. "She knew not that I gave her corn, and wine, and oil . . ." (v. 8). God is the giver of every good gift; the fount and source of all benefit and blessing. Whenever His people turn from Him, they abjure their own highest good, as well as His covenant grace. All who forsake the Lord are blind and foolish; their anticipated pleasures will prove to be but a mirage; their expected "land of plenty" a barren wilderness (2:11–13).

Worship of the false gods of materialism, self-indulgence and pleasure never fully satisfies, but leaves an aching void—the "vanity" and emptiness so eloquently described by the Preacher in Ecclesiastes. In the ultimate, God will not be mocked: and all those who turn from Him will at last find—all too bitterly—that He has finally turned from them (2:13).

Thus Hosea learned, in his home and the sorrows of his family life, the full implications and effects of Israel's apostasy. He was thus able to describe more movingly than any other prophet the true character of spiritual adultery, and its dire consequences. Those realities of human and of divine relationship are as valid today as when Hosea wrote his book 2,700 years ago.

4

Love's Ultimate Expression

DESPITE the fateful flaws in Gomer's character, which so soon led her into becoming "a wife of whoredoms," Hosea's marriage doubtless began with true love on his part, high aspirations and glowing hopes. Yet, greedy for gain, she played the harlot—and thereby acted toward her devoted husband as apostate Israel behaved toward God. The most loving husband, no matter how sorely wounded he might be, will not stand idly observant of such conduct: every effort must be made to check it. "Therefore, behold, I will hedge up thy way with thorns, and make a wall, that she shall not find her paths" (2 : 6). Because of her sin Gomer—and Israel—will be checked in her wicked ways. Moreover, the good things on which she sets such store will be taken from her (2 : 9). That these two acts of chastisement are a direct consequence of her sin, is indicated by the repeated "therefore" (2:6, 9).

Then, in v. 14, we have a third "therefore." This is one of the most arresting verses in the book. Surely it will pronounce a third judgment; a final stroke; a decisive hammer blow! Not so; instead of a climax in chastisement is something startlingly unexpected—the paradox of divine grace. At the revealing of the extremity of sin, deserving severest judgment, is the pronouncement of mercy, "I will allure her . . . and speak comfortably (literally, '*to the heart*') unto her . . ." The only possible comment upon this astounding verse is the equally stupendous statement of the apostle, "Where sin abounded, grace did much more abound."

Forgiveness of sin, however, while given freely on God's part, is never unconditional, or thrust upon those who spurn it. And so, in order to bring an unfaithful wife—and a wayward people—to a sense of need, "I will bring her into the wilderness . . ."—into a bleak and barren place—not to break the spirit and bend the will, but rather in order to "speak to the heart." How often God needs to separate His people from the distractions and busy-ness of the world, into a "wilderness," to manifest, not His indignation, but His love. Then, man's extremity so often proves to be God's opportunity; and in a place of dearth and well-nigh despair, He gives "the valley of Achor for a door of hope" (2:15).

The valley of Achor was a place of solemn significance for Israel. It was for ever associated with the stern judgment of God upon sin. Israel, after the great victory over Jericho, was stunned when its army was defeated by the insignificant little town of Ai. Prostrate before God, its leader Joshua learned the reason for this discomfiture—the sin of Achan, in disobeying the command and defying the will of God concerning the spoils of Jericho. The onward march of Israel was halted until judgment was executed—as it was in the valley of Achor, where Achan and his family paid the penalty of their greed and folly, by being stoned. This incident became a classic example to the nation of the consequences of sin and the penalty of disobedience to God's law. The very name of the valley of Achor became expressive of the inexorable standards of the divine judgment.

This place of sombre association, however, is now—like Jezreel—given a new and glorious significance: it shall become "a door of hope." The place of sin and defeat and condemnation shall become, through the pardoning mercy of God, the gateway into possession of His promises to His people. The very place of judgment is transformed into the scene of renewal of vows and of restored love. "It shall be at that day, saith the Lord, that thou shalt call me *Ishi* ('my husband') and shalt no more call me *Baali* ('my lord')." There will be a full response on the part of His people to His covenant grace, and glad embracing of the privileged relationship to which He calls them. And an evidence of the reality of this change of heart will be a putting away of the things that defile (2:17).

The Lord holds out to His people, if only they will repent and return, a threefold pledge—"I will betroth thee unto me" . . . for ever; in righteousness; and in faithfulness (2 : 19, 20): the absolute affirmation of the Triune God. Instead of scattering in judgment (Jezreel, 2 : 22), there will be "sowing" into blessing (2 : 23): the pledge of fruitfulness, for their enjoyment and for His glory.

The final verse of Hosea 2, "I will have mercy upon her that had not obtained mercy; and I will say to them which were not my people, Thou art my people; and they shall say, Thou art my God," is quoted by the apostle Paul in Romans 9 : 25–26, concerning God's future purposes for Israel: there is, for His earthly people, a fulfilment of this prophecy which is still to come. He is faithful who promises, and will yet redeem and restore the covenant nation of Israel. We, however, who through faith are heirs of the promises, have no need to wait for future realisation of the blessedness here proclaimed. We can enjoy *now*, in all its abiding reality, the glad assurance that we are His and He is ours.

Future prospect gave way for Hosea, however, to present problems, as he returned in chapter 3 to his travail over Gomer. In this short chapter the drama of his unfaltering love for his wanton wife—and God's for Israel—reaches its astounding climax. In order to plumb the depths of the sorrow of God concerning faithless Israel, Hosea had to face the fact of his wife's utter degradation—and then go and seek her, in order to lift her up again from the mire, and restore her to her family and station. Here, presented most poignantly in the personal experience of the prophet, we glimpse something of the matchless, patient, persistent love of God. We see also the length to which He will go in order to win back again the most degraded and unworthy. Moreover we are assured that, despite the ravages of apostasy and sin, His purposes will ultimately triumph over all the allurements and power of evil.

In his dejection and despair at Gomer's disloyalty, Hosea was commanded by God, "Go yet, love a woman beloved of her friend, yet an adulteress . . ." (3:1). This verse has occasioned perplexity and even controversy among Bible students, as to its exact meaning. It is generally agreed, however, that the "friend" is not her paramour; rather God is calling Hosea to prove himself her true friend in her desperate plight, despite the hurt and humiliation she has caused him. Knowing full well that she was still an adulteress, the forsaken husband is commanded to seek her out and show her what *true* love really is. Love that would go to the ultimate lengths of expression in tender word and gracious deed. That alone could reach and melt her cold, calculating heart, and win her back from her depravity.

This was the hardest thing that God could require of Hosea—of any husband—toward an unfaithful wife. Only the realisation that God not only understood and entered into his travail, but was by it revealing something of His own, could give Hosea the grace and strength to obey. God was asking of Hosea more than any man could be expected to do: but *He* was doing this toward apostate Israel, and should not Hosea act accordingly toward Gomer?

The unfaithful wife had forfeited his love, by spurning and forsaking it. But nothing less than love would suffice to win her back.

It would not be enough to seek her out and show compassion—a readiness to forgive. Those most desperately needing forgiveness are all too often suspicious of it; for forgiveness can be offered in a spirit of self-righteousness which makes its acceptance impossible. Hosea was to show forth, in his whole manner and being, as well as in word and deed, true love to her, although she had not been true to him; love warm, tender, unwavering. In our human experience we often see love, rejected, turn into scorn; bitter disappointment develop into hatred. But not with God!

Here we have illustrated one of the most important lessons of the entire Scriptures concerning the seeking and saving of the lost. Nothing less than the love of God shed abroad in the heart will suffice to constrain us to stoop to the lowest and neediest, in a manner which will win their confidence and evoke their response. Nothing less than a love kindled by His own, will prevail.

In obeying this command, Hosea was reminded that he would enter into a fellowship of suffering and of redemptive ministry with God Himself. This was brought home to him by the remarkable statement that such action would be "according to the love of the Lord toward the children of Israel, who look to other gods, and love flagons of wine"—or rather, "cakes of raisins" (*RV*), referring to the dried grapes used in Baal ritual. Gomer and Israel were behaving precisely alike—Gomer with her "lovers," and Israel with false gods.

So Hosea sought Gomer, and eventually found her in the slave-market. Her greedy desires and hopes of gain had led her here! Such is the deceitfulness of sin: it promises the skies and leads to the dunghill. Degraded, despised, utterly destitute; forsaken by those she had so foolishly thought to be her friends. They had used her for their own pleasure and profit, and then discarded her.

"So I bought her . . ." the record runs, in simple and unadorned phrase: but what drama lies behind the words! He bought—*redeemed*—her; and to do so cost him *everything he had*. The price of a slave in those days was twenty pieces of silver (Gen. 37:28); apparently Hosea possessed only fifteen pieces, and had to make up the balance with an homer-and-half of barley. He had to give his all, to buy back again to himself his unfaithful wife.

We too have been redeemed; and at infinite cost. Not with silver and gold, or any corruptible thing: nothing less than the precious blood of Christ could avail for our purchase-price. God had to give

His only-begotten Son; Jesus had to give His life, a ransom for the many.

Even when delivered from her shame and slavery, Gomer could not be restored immediately to her place in the family and home: "Thou shalt abide for me many days . . ." (3 : 3). There must be a time of separation, of cleansing and restoration. Forgiveness for the repentant is full and free; but the effects of apostasy, the entail of sin, are not always eliminated in a day. It sometimes takes quite a while to get back into the place we so foolishly forsook in our experience of backsliding. But the ultimate realisation of all God's purposes of grace is assured. "Afterwards shall the children of Israel return, and seek the Lord their God . . . and shall fear the Lord and His goodness in the latter days" (v. 5).

Estrangement from God is the greatest tragedy any Christian can experience; it inflicts immeasurable sorrow upon God, and incalculable evil upon the wayward. Hosea's story and message bring urgent summons to repent and return, while assuring us of the unwavering love of the One we have so sorely wounded. Never were Hosea's vicarious suffering, and his prophetic ministry, more relevant than they are today.

5

Divine Indictment

WHEN a sovereign speaks, his people heed, and hasten to obey. When God, the high and holy, sovereign Lord of heaven and earth, makes known His will, surely all His creatures—who derive life and breath and all things from Him—will be swift to respond. So anyone would think, who knew nothing of history and of the human heart! It is the most astounding fact, surely, both of divine revelation and of everyday experience, that mankind whom He made in His own image and likeness, for the satisfaction of His deepest heart-need and for His supreme eternal glory, should become predominantly defiant, degraded, regardless of His Person and claims.

This startling situation is indicated in the very first word of Hosea's prophetic utterances. His series of public pronouncements, beginning in chapter 4, opens with the arresting call, "Hear the word of the Lord, ye children of Israel. . . ." In his own bitter sorrow, "the word of the Lord" had come to Hosea; now, his personal experience having become the means of understanding the nation's harlotry in relation to God, he is impelled to proclaim the Almighty's indictment of an apostate people.

The sting of Hosea's challenge, and the poignancy of the situation, lie in the fact that it is the "children of Israel" whom he addresses. Not the world at large, but the privileged people of God; the recipients of His especial care and bounty, to whom had been given the oracles and ordinances of covenant relationship and grace. It was *His own people* who turned from the living and true God to idols; from His holy temple to pagan high place and ritual; from walking in His ways to every imaginable evil.

In that, they were all too characteristic of practically every generation of the children of Israel under the old covenant, and of the professing church under the new. This challenge to hear the word of the Lord sounds throughout the entire Scriptures, Old Testament and New alike. God spoke through law-giver, psalmist and prophets; and for the most part, the people paid scant attention.

The constant call of the messengers of the Lord was that the nation should *hearken*.

In these last days God has spoken, fully and finally, in His Son, the Word incarnate. His reiterated exhortation, in the days of His flesh, was, "He that hath ears to hear, let him hear"; and finally, in most solemn peroration to the messages to the seven churches, He adjures His new-covenant people, "He that hath an ear, let him hear what the Spirit saith to the churches." We have no excuse if *we* fail to heed and to obey.

Hosea's message to Israel was that "The Lord hath a controversy with the inhabitants of the land" (4 : 1). The accusation was not based, in the first instance, on religious grounds, but moral and social—"there is no truth nor mercy . . . in the land." This was due, however, to the fact that there was no "knowledge of God" (4 : 1). Spiritual factors lie at the heart of moral and social problems. Relationship to God determines conduct among men. Departure from faith in God and loyalty to Him, leads inescapably to breakdown in standards of behaviour—swearing, lying, killing, stealing, committing adultery and murder, in Britain today, as in Israel when Hosea prophesied (4 : 2).

The entire life of a nation is affected by the sin of its people (4 : 3). Hosea brings this home with a startling illustration. "I will not punish your daughters when they play the harlot," God says, "nor your brides when they commit adultery: for the men themselves go aside with harlots, and sacrifice with cult prostitutes" (4 : 14, *RSV*). Moral standards collapse when spiritual values are forsaken, and when the gods of the world are given the place which should be the Lord's alone. The self-indulgence of the younger generation is not so much their fault as that of those who fail to set them a right example; for had the right standards been maintained by the parents, the children would not so easily have erred. The blame rests primarily upon those who wantonly depart from God, His law, His house and revealed will.

Worst of all, it is useless to strive against this state of affairs, for sinners cannot amend the ways of sinners (4 : 4)! This is a most relevant fact to face today. Departure from faith in our nation has resulted in the highest-ever crime figures, blatant immorality, increase in drug addiction, the betting and gambling fever, and declining standards generally. So alarming is the situation that even Humanists are endeavouring to re-establish some of the abandoned "codes of Christian conduct" and to inspire more lofty ideals. Their attempts are futile. Once foundations are shaken, the buttressing of buildings is unavailing.

The supreme tragedy is, that those who could and should speak to the condition of the people—the priest and the prophet—all too often fail in their awsomely responsible task (4 : 4–5); for sadly, it is too commonly true that "like people, like priest" (v. 9). Instead of being exemplary people, walking with God and His witnesses to the nation, the "priests" tend to become conformed to the spirit, outlook and habits of the age. Indeed, Hosea charged those of his day with exploiting the prevailing conditions for their own gain (4 : 8). Professionalism is ever the bane of religion and the antagonist of true godliness. Solemn judgment is, therefore, pronounced upon the unfaithful priests; for their failure is commensurate with their privilege and responsibility: "I will punish them," says the Lord, "for their ways, and requite them for their deeds" (4 : 9).

It is significant that the prophet attributes this state of affairs to *lack of knowledge of God* (4 : 6). We might ask, How could this be, since the people of Israel had surely been familiar from earliest childhood with His law and ordinances? Intellectually, yes: but Hosea makes clear that behind this façade of superficial acquaintance with the word and will of God, there was no true understanding; no love and trust and loyalty; no realisation of relationship, through covenant grace, with the Most High.

There is a "knowledge" which is worse than the profoundest ignorance; a profession which, instead of benefiting, condemns the one who makes it—a shallow cognizance of certain facts about God, which might easily be mistaken, both by the person possessing it and by others, for true intimacy with Him. Therein lies its peril: it can deceive and delude its possessor into thinking he *knows* God, when, in fact, there is gravest ignorance of Him.

That was the tragedy of Israel; that is the plight of so large a proportion of the professing church today. Knowledge *about* God; regular attendance at church services; even study of the Scriptures, are not necessarily the same thing as knowledge of the Lord. The New Testament is insistent upon the necessity of the "full knowledge" available to us in and through Christ; and the apostle Paul expressed the response we all should make—"That I might *know him. . . .*" (Phil. 3 : 10).

Such lack of knowledge as led Israel to its doom—and imperils the church today—is blameworthy, wilful ignorance; quite different in character and consequences from the unenlightened state of those who have had no opportunity to hear and understand: those upon whom the light of the Gospel has not shined. When divine revelation is deliberately set aside and superstition embraced; when mere ceremonial is substituted for worship in spirit and in truth, then the ensuing estrangement from God is culpable indeed. Then Beth-el becomes Beth-aven; the House of God degenerates into a House of vanity (4 : 15).

Finally in this chapter, Hosea turns momentarily from Ephraim to give a side-long glance and warning to the southern kingdom of Judah: "Though you play the harlot, O Israel, let not Judah become guilty . . ." (4 : 15). The apostasy of the northern kingdom had reached a pitch which rendered the people totally captive to the idols they had embraced: "Ephraim is joined to idols; let him alone" (4 : 17). There is a state of hardness in sin which seals the destiny of those involved. There is also a limit to the constraints of divine grace and the call of love. It is not for us to define that limit: we might impose it where God does not; but there is clear warning in Scripture that "my Spirit shall not always strive with man" (Gen. 6 : 3).

There are, however, differences of degree in loyalty and disloyalty, devotion and backsliding. Judah was by no means blameless, and in due course was given into captivity; but whereas Israel was virtually blotted out as a nation, and eliminated from the on-going purposes of God, Judah was preserved and has continued through all the vicissitudes of the centuries as the distinctive covenant race.

The warning to Judah underlines, however, the peril of conformity to the spirit of the age: the tendency of the human heart to follow pernicious examples. It is never easy to walk in fellowship with God and in righteousness before men; it is especially difficult "amid a crooked and perverse generation." Such, however, was Judah's high calling; and such is ours today. We can do so only as we cherish the reality of abiding relationship with the Lord, by the Spirit, nourished and guided by His Word.

6

Priests, People and King

HAVING begun his prophetic ministry with a call to Israel to "Hear the word of the Lord" (4 : 1), Hosea repeated the call more insistently in his second message—only this time he addressed it to the priests, people and king, in threefold summons—

> Hear this, O priests!
> Give heed, O house of Israel!
> Hearken, O house of the king! (5 : 1).

Not only was it more specific in address; the prophetic message was more severe in tone, for it declared not merely that the Lord had a controversy with them, but that "judgment pertains to you . . ." This was the consequence of their rejection of the word of the Lord: God had repeatedly given them warning and exhortation, through several prophets; but they had disregarded—and seemingly with impunity, for God is ever reluctant to bring judgment upon even the most erring. They misunderstood the long-suffering of God, however, and presumed further upon His compassionate patience; they assumed that the threatened judgment would never fall upon them, and that they could safely continue to ignore the divine admonitions.

Now their "cup of iniquity" was full, and it was Hosea's task to tell them that the uplifted sword was about to strike. For Ephraim, the hour of doom was at hand; yet they behaved as if the prophet's warnings were mere froth and folly, and as if judgment would never come. The self-same tragedy is for ever being re-enacted: God's admonitions are unheeded, and His subsequent visitations unexpected although so clearly foretold.

So it will be in the greatest judgment-day of all, when grace has run its full course and the rejected Saviour ascends the great white throne. Despite every warning, the nations will be astonished when the last trump sounds. Perhaps the Lord's true spokesmen of today fulfil for their generation the rôle which Hosea did for his.

Once more a specific indictment is brought against the priests; and to it is added one against the king—for privilege and prestige are ever accompanied by commensurate accountability. It is probable that the king alluded to was Pekah (2 Kings 15 : 25–31; cf. Isa. 7 : 1); and the charge against him was, "You have been a snare at Mizpah, and a net spread upon Tabor" (5 : 1). Mizpah and Tabor were "high places" east and west of Jordan respectively, where the king had, like a hunter, entrapped the people by encouraging them to indulge in his idolatrous practices. The especial guilt of the priests and king does not, however, absolve the people who followed their bad example: for people are not sheep. Israel had the law of God and knew His will; but of their own choice they followed the evil ways of their leaders. They are therefore joined with them in the threefold judgment of God.

In His messages to the seven churches of Asia, the ascended Lord indicated that the basis of judgment upon professing people of God is the same under the new covenant as under the old—His intimate and thorough knowledge of them, as they intrinsically *are,* as distinct from what they profess, and might appear to others to be. "I know thy works," said He who walked among the seven lampstands; and here, "I know Ephraim, and Israel is not hid from me . . ." (5 : 3). Whereas they were in their sorry state through lack of knowledge of the Lord, He affirms His absolute knowledge of them—to their undoing: for "O Ephraim, thou committest whoredom, and Israel is defiled." Not only king and priests, but the entire people are brought within the compass of the divine indictment.

One of the most solemn facts revealed in the Scriptures is that men, by their deliberate choice in the crucial matters of relationship to God and obedience to His will, fix their characters and determine their destiny. We all know how people become "set in their ways." So it is spiritually. There comes a time when they seem irrevocably bound by the course of life they have followed, so that they are unable to alter even if they would—as Romans 6 : 16 affirms, "Know ye not that to whom ye yield yourselves servants to obey, his servants ye are to whom ye obey; whether of sin unto death, or of obedience unto righteousness?" We would, of course, set no limits to the divine grace or the transforming power of the Saviour; but all experience testifies that far fewer people are converted in later life than in youth. Some seem utterly impervious to the influences of the Gospel; they have hardened their hearts so long and so persistently that it seems as if those hearts are turned to stone.

That was Israel's condition. "Their deeds do not permit them to return to their God. For the spirit of harlotry is within them . . ." (5 : 4). God had become to them a meaningless irrelevance: they had no desire for fellowship with Him. Instead, they were held captive by—and delighted in—the "spirit of harlotry."

Notice that the prophetic word penetrates beneath the surface of their indulgences in idolatry, to the "spirit of harlotry" which animated them: for behind and beneath all false beliefs and practices are spiritual factors. Centuries later, the apostle Paul affirmed that the most sinister aspect of idol worship is that those who indulge in it are not merely sacrificing to wood and stone, but submitting themselves to the authority of evil spirits (1 Cor. 10 : 20). So those who turn from the things of God to the world, thereby yield themselves captive to the spirit of the world, the spirit of the age, and come—whether they recognise the fact or not—under the authority of the prince of this age, the devil.

It is no light matter to reject the Gospel, in the quest for a "good time": millions of people are lightheartedly submitting to a spiritual domination of which they are totally unaware. Indeed, if warned of it, the very existence of those spiritual factors would be spurned as "pure imagination," in much the same way as Hosea's warnings were by his contemporaries.

No man can ever allege, however, that he has been doomed without warning. God's Word goes out to all; the merits of the redemptive sacrifice of Christ are available to all; the constraints of His Spirit are upon all: it is in spite of love's utmost effort that any are judged. But love rejected, must condemn. "The pride of Israel doth testify to his face" (5 : 5). Therein lies one of the puzzles of the book: does this word "pride" refer to God, or to their sin? Is it a term coined by the prophet as a name for God—the One in whom they should boast; or is Hosea affirming that their pride—echoing the primeval sin—rises up and arraigns them? It can be taken either way, though a majority of Bible expositors prefer the latter interpretation.

In this pronouncement of penalty, Judah is joined to Israel: "therefore shall Israel and Ephraim fall in their iniquity; Judah also shall fall with them." Alas that apostasy is so infectious; evil example is so potent! But Judah could not blame Israel for its own participation in evil: each stands on his own feet and is answerable for his own behaviour. It was Judah's sin which God would judge, as well as Ephraim's. The fact that others may be worse offenders than we—violent sinners, whereas we are moderate, even "respectable"—does not absolve us: for *all* have sinned, and come short of the glory of God.

Nor is a "panic repentance" in the day of evil of any avail. "With their flocks and herds they shall go to seek the Lord; but they will not find Him; He has withdrawn from them" (5:6). God is not a mere convenience, on whose benevolence we can call whenever we are in a desperate plight. Nor will He be bribed by our prayers and promises in such an hour. There comes a time when grace has run its course: the "day of rebuke" has come (5 : 9)! Upon Israel, judgment was ministered through the invading Assyrians. Then indeed was Israel desolate: for Assyria was a pitiless conqueror.

The day of judgment was heralded by a trumpet blast (5:8). So shall be the final judgment—only then, the last trumpet will be sounded by the archangel. Two striking and seemingly conflicting metaphors are used to illustrate the judgment of God—"I will be unto Ephraim as a moth . . ." (5:12); and "I will be unto Ephraim as a lion . . ." (5:14). These are, in fact, not so incompatible as they seem: they indicate two aspects of the activity of God. He brings about His purposes quietly and over a period of time, like the unobserved action of the moth; He also roars and devours in a moment.

Judgment, His strange act and terrible work, is both a process and a climactic event. Israel was all unconsciously already experiencing the disintegration of national life, the inward workings of corruption, the sapping of strength and spoliation of covenant relationship with God; and it would face the stark reality of all this when the Assyrian invaded the land and carried the people away captive. Likewise the pronouncements of the Scriptures concerning the last days are being outwrought silently and persistently here and now, and will be manifest in majestic leonine "roar" at the end of the age.

Another sidelight on the interplay between human action and divine overruling is indicated in 5:13. "When Ephraim saw his sickness, and Judah saw his wound, then Ephraim went to Assyria, and sent to the great king. But he is not able to cure you or heal your wound." In the time of extremity, those who should have trusted in the Lord their God turned to the world—and it proved to be the instrument of judgment, rather than of deliverance. There is also for His people now, as then, no other Saviour than the Lord: all else will prove but scourges and scorpions.

Perhaps the most pertinent part of the prophecies of Hosea to the church in our own day and generation lies in the "asides" addressed to Judah. The southern kingdom, although tainted with similar sins to those of the north, nevertheless never went so far as to forfeit covenant relationship with God: but it was admonished and chastened for its wrongdoings. Here, amid the pronouncement of doom upon Israel, is a stern word to Judah—"The princes of Judah have become like those who remove the landmark; upon them will I pour out my wrath like water" (5:10).

In the time of travail for Israel, apparently Judah saw an opportunity of seizing some of the territory of the northern kingdom, and could not resist the temptation to grab. In His rebuke, God insists that His law is immutable, and that right conduct must be observed at all times. The fact that affairs in Israel were in a state of flux did not warrant illicit action on the part of Judah. Right is right and wrong is wrong, whatever the prevailing circumstances —and despite the human tendency to take advantage of another's discomfiture. Events do not affect principles; prevailing evils do not justify the people of God in committing other wrongs. They must act rightly and righteously at all times; must maintain the standards and observe the laws of God even if earthly law and order break down. If they fail to do so, God says, the conditions of which they endeavour to take advantage will descend upon them also. Having declared that He would "be unto Ephraim as a lion," the Lord added, "and as a young lion to the house of Judah." If we would escape the condemnation of the ungodly, we must beware not to partake of their deeds.

The last word of God, however, up to the very crack of doom, is ever winsome and appealing; there is a way of repentance and restoration right until the stroke of midnight. "I will go and return to my place," He says, through the prophet, "till they acknowledge their offence, and seek my face." To the earnest seeker, He is ever available: there is, through Christ, an open way of access into His presence . . . and no matter what sin has been indulged or whoredom has defiled, all who truly seek Him will find Him to be the God of pardoning mercy and redeeming grace.

7

Feigned Repentance

In response to the indictment of God through Hosea, Israel made a profession of repentance which, on the surface, seems so genuine that it is often cited as a model of contrition and return to the Lord on the part of backsliders—

> "Come, let us return to the Lord;
> for He has torn, that He may heal us;
> He has stricken, and He will bind us up.
> After two days He will revive us;
> on the third day He will raise us up,
> that we may live before Him" (6 : 1–2, *RSV*).

These words seem to have the ring of true penitence; of humble petition for pardoning grace. So persuasive are they that Dr. C. I. Scofield heads this section, in his Bible, "The voice of the remnant in the last days"—though incidentally, what this passage has to do with the "last days" baffles comprehension: Scofield's heading is an example of his brand of dispensationalism run riot.

Why, it might be asked, do we cast doubt on the sincerity of the sentiments expressed? The answer is clear and plain: because God does so! Perhaps there is no verse in Scripture more revealing of the emotions of God concerning His wayward people (if we may use this anthropomorphic term in relation to Him), than this—

> What shall I do with you, O Ephraim?
> What shall I do with you, O Judah?
> Your love is like a morning cloud,
> like the dew that goes early away (6 : 4).

Here we see mingled the wounded love and disappointed hopes of God: the wistful yearning for honest repentance on the part of Israel, yet the pained realisation that this profession did not ring true. The words sprang too easily from their lips; they did not come from the heart. Israel's repentance was superficial; their avowal of renewed loyalty to the Lord was feigned. Indeed, the manner of their approach to God indicates the shallowness of their profession of penitence: there is no sorrow for sin in it; no recognition of hurt inflicted upon the Lord; no acknowledgment of guilt. There is a too easy asumption that God will at once receive them with open arms: "He has torn, that He may heal us; He has stricken, and He will bind us up"—almost as if He were blameworthy, not they! Superficial views regarding sin lead always to shallow conceptions of its consequences.

Those who have any understanding whatsoever of the character of God, and of the heinousness of sin, can never regard repentance as a light and easy matter; restoration as a mere kiss of forgiveness. Estrangement from God is never occasioned by His act, but ours: it is sin that separates. That barrier is never broken down by a facile "I'm sorry"!

One of the great dangers of enlightenment in Scriptural truth lies in the placing of undue emphasis upon any one aspect of the divine revelation, rather than holding the entire word of God in proper balance. God is love: that is true, for His word declares it. But it is not the whole truth about His Personality, and His attitude toward erring mankind: the word also reveals Him as holy and righteous, a God of undeviating demands and of inexorable judgment. Those who too lightly—today, as in Hosea's generation—assume that His love must express itself in an easy-going attitude toward sin, and an eager readiness to restore the wayward the moment they make conciliatory gestures, are profoundly mistaken.

Israel's eloquently phrased "repentance" was of this character; and it did not deceive the Lord. "Your love," He said, "is like a morning cloud, like the dew that goes early away" (6:4). Mere words; entirely on the surface, not penetrating to the roots of the problem. There is, however, a music in words which can capture the mind like magic; which can lure and lull both the speaker and hearer into believing that such mellifluous speech must of necessity produce the desired result.

How tragically mistaken this can be! For what could be more pleasing to the ear, more beguiling to the mind, and more deceptive to the spirit than this—

> Let us know, let us press on to know the Lord;
> His going forth is sure as the dawn;
> He will come to us as the showers,
> as the spring rains that water the earth (6 : 3).

Such beauty of speech would deceive the very elect into thinking that this was true spirituality and inspired utterance. Alas, impeccable as the words are, they are worthless if spoken solely with the lips and not from the heart—and God knew that in this instance they lacked the value which heartfelt sincerity alone could impart.

It is always easy to discern and discuss the folly and failures of others; it is easier still to be blind to the self-same errors in ourselves. It is perhaps the paramount weakness of Evangelicals today to confuse a shrewd perception of truth and error with a *living-out* of truth; to substitute the use of correct terminology for the reality of Christian faith and practice. We assume that, if we subscribe to sound doctrine; if we affirm the right formulae in the right tone of voice, then we are loyal to the truth and well-pleasing to God.

The test established by our Lord, however, was far more searching: "By their *fruits*," He said, concerning those who professed to be His disciples, "ye shall know them." The bounteous provisions of the new covenant are pledged to those whose lives are truly submitted to the Lordship of Christ, rather than to those who merely mouth correct phrases. God is never deluded by mere words, and these honeyed statements of the people of Israel in Hosea's day did not deceive Him.

"Therefore," God proceeded—in expression of that inexorable judgment to which we have referred—"I have hewn them by the prophets; I have slain them by the words of my mouth . . ." (6:5). As hypocritical profession is abhorrent to Him, so also is mere ceremonial and religious observance. "For I desire steadfast love, and not sacrifice: the knowledge of God, rather than burnt offerings" (6 : 6). God reads the hearts, and knows the deepest intent of the being; and He requires practical proof of true godliness in character and conduct.

There is a penetrating thrust in the observation regarding the words of the prophets; for by His messengers God both called the people to penitence and pronounced doom upon them if they failed to heed. But note that God speaks as if His words were deeds—"I *have hewn* them by the prophets; I *have slain* them by the words of my mouth . . ." The effect is inevitable; in the purpose of God, it is already accomplished. No word of God can fail of total fulfilment.

It is the most awesome thing in the world to hear the word of God. By it we live—or eternally perish. There is life in the word;

or condemnation and death. And the word of the prophet is the word of God. Preachers of the Gospel speak forth that which brings eternal life, or the second death. Ultimate issues lie in the proclaiming—and hearing—of the word of God.

While the condemnation of Israel's backsliding and hypocrisy was pronounced against the entire nation, God pin-pointed certain specific sins, particular places and individual sinners: "Gilead is a city of evildoers, and is polluted with blood . . ." (6:8). Gilead! The name is associated in the minds of many readers of the Bible with one of the most intriguing of OT verses—"Is there no balm in Gilead?" This brief question educes thoughts of healing, of emollient for wounds, of restoring grace. Here, however, very different emotions are evoked; and Gilead, instead of having a pleasing and hopeful sound, takes on an ominous note.

Once more the prophet arraigns the priests especially: "As robbers lie in wait for a man, so the priests are banded together; they murder . . . yea, they commit villainy" (6:9). The degradation of the noblest is always the supreme tragedy, and the sin of those occupying holy office is the most heinous.

This leads Hosea to the climax of his series of solemn charges in this chapter: "In the house of Israel I have seen a horrible thing; Ephraim's harlotry is there" (6 : 10). Harlotry: the word sums up his indictment. Born out of Hosea's own family tragedy and his personal sorrow, "harlotry"—or "whoredom" (*AV*) expresses the abhorrent character of the nation's sin, and the travail it inflicts upon the Almighty, the betrayed Husband and Lord of His covenant people. "Israel," the prophet declares, "is defiled."

Where is now the easy optimism, the feigned repentance of the opening verses of the chapter? Superficial profession is exposed in its true light; the cold, calculating, unchanged heart of the people is fully revealed, as seen by the all-searching eye of the Lord.

Then, finally, the prophet once more turns aside from Ephraim to Judah, and utters a further short, sharp admonition to the southern kingdom. Let none rejoice in, or be unmoved by, the judgment of God upon others, he warns; for He is the Lord and the Judge of us all, and we all must stand one day before His judgment seat.

8

A Cake Not Turned

AN interesting characteristic of Hosea's literary style is a rare skill in using graphic metaphors and apposite epigrams, which convey his message most arrestingly. These parables in miniature undoubtedly made considerable impact upon the minds of his hearers; and they would linger in their memories, for such vivid word-pictures are not soon forgotten. How often a felicitous illustration in a sermon will remain with us, long after the substance of the address is wiped from memory. Hosea well knew this secret of effective preaching. We have already encountered some of his pithy sayings. It was he who coined the phrase, "like people, like priest" (4:9); he conjures up a ludicrous mental image with the words, "Israel slideth back as a backsliding heifer"—we can see in the mind's eye the silly beast slithering on a muddy slope (4:16); again, "I will be unto Ephraim as a moth . . . as a lion" (5:12, 14); and "Your goodness is as a morning cloud, and as the early dew . . ." (6:4). The full flowering of this facility comes in chapter 7, where Hosea uses four telling metaphors to bring home to the people of Israel the enormity of their sin—an over-heated oven; a cake not turned; sapped strength and gray hairs of which they are unaware; and "Ephraim is a silly dove without a heart."

Once again the Lord stresses, through the prophet, that in His mercy He is ready to rescind the impending judgment if only they will repent. "When I would heal Israel, the corruption of Ephraim is revealed, and the wicked deeds of Samaria . . ." (7 : 1). A pause in the threatening and aggressive activities of Assyria gave Israel a breathing-space in which to seek the Lord: instead, they went headlong into self-indulgence and sin. They couldn't recognise the opportunity afforded them by divine grace; rather, they were captured and constrained by their own inclinations and wicked ways. If they treated the matter so lightheartedly, however, God did not: "They do not consider that I remember all their evil works. Now their deeds encompass them; they are before my face" (7:2). The prophet goes on to describe scenes of abandoned revelling and licentiousness. The excesses of the populace equal those of the king's court: they vie with one another in iniquity, and take delight in the sinfulness they share (7:3–4). Some special occasion of national revelry is indicated in v. 5, "In the day of our king the princes have made him sick with the heat of wine; he stretched out his hand with scorners." Ellison, however, grappling with the very corrupt Hebrew text, suggests that the real meaning of the passage has been "veiled by a number of scribal errors," and that "verse 7 makes it clear that . . . it was not the rulers themselves who are the point of the oracle, but the men responsible for their destruction and murder."

All this leads up to the parable of the baker and his oven (7:6–7). Some obscurity in the text has occasioned diversity in its interpretation; but the picture unmistakably emerges of a deliberate and determined self-giving to evil, and of a fevered preoccupation with that evil—the piling of fuel on the fire, so that it gets hotter and hotter.

Here are two pertinent lessons for today, as well as for Hosea's generation. No one enters upon a sinful pattern and course of life without choosing to do so; but those making such a choice become prisoners of the sins they indulge, and are eventually driven by passions and forces of evil beyond their original intent. There is a potency in sin which enslaves the will and dominates the personality and directs the actions of those who thought to use it for their own pleasure and purposes. "Know ye not," said the apostle Paul, centuries later, "that to whom ye yield yourselves servants to obey, his servants ye are to whom ye obey; whether of sin unto death, or of obedience unto righteousness?" (Rom. 6:16).

There is the driving, destructive power of *fire* in sin, compelling its victims to obey its behests, and then impelling them to their doom. How awesome a fact this is, if only men and women would wake up to it! How urgently we should re-echo the prophet's admonition in our day, when on every hand we witness the breakdown of moral standards, when sexual lust literally burns "as a flaming fire" (7:6), and even professing Christians indulge the "new morality." Old sins by new names do not deceive the Lord, no matter how much they might delude their foolish dupes. When sins and sinners are "hot as an oven," let us proclaim with prophetic voice that the anger of the Lord against such iniquity is hotter than any oven, no matter how much it might be over-heated: and from *that* flame there will be no escaping!

More graphic still is Hosea's parable of "a cake not turned." The picture is, of course, of a flat griddle-cake, scorched on one side but uncooked on the other; nauseous and utterly ruined. The immediate application was probably to Israel's excessive worldly-wisdom in trying to play off Assyria and Egypt, the two great rival powers, by proposing treaties with each—instead of trusting in the Lord. Confidence in such half-baked diplomacy rather than trust in God, had resulted in the stench of scorching—for Egypt and Assyria both saw through their manœuvrings and treated them accordingly; while their lack of reliance upon the Lord was even more foolish. The result was an Israel utterly abhorrent to God—and to the nations they sought to placate.

A cake not turned: what a picture of a people, a life, ruined by over-indulgence in one respect, or over-emphasis upon one aspect of life at the expense of that balance which is so constantly set forth in Scripture! The late Dr. D. M. M'Intyre used to impress upon his students the axiom, "Keep to the middle of the King's Highway"—and one at least has cherished that counsel as a guiding principle of life.

We see on every hand the folly and frustration of becoming "a cake not turned." How many lives fail to attain their full potentialities through lack of balance: some failing or prejudice or oddity makes them lop-sided and unreliable. In spiritual matters, how tragic it is when intellectualism subdues faith; when creed outshines conduct; or ritualism supplants true worship.

On this matter, however, we would remind ourselves again that it is easy to see the faults of others; difficult to discern our own. Among Evangelicals there is many a "cake not turned." Wherever there is over-emphasis upon one aspect of truth, this danger exists. Some, for instance, stress the Spirit-directed wisdom of the Reformers, almost as if their teaching has virtually equal authority to that of the apostles. The Reformers themselves, convinced as they were of the rightness of their stand for the truth, would nevertheless have been the first to reject vigorously any claims for inspiration or authority apart from that which they derived from the Scriptures. Again, others revere the Puritans in a way which exalts their writings almost to a parity with the New Testament. These devotees would be horror-struck to realise that they regard the Puritan literature in much the same way as the Roman church regards its "tradition"—but such is the fact. Certain Pentecostal teaching, extreme dispensationalism, and doctrines of "eradication"

—these and other excesses are all instances in our midst of "a cake not turned."

Repeatedly Hosea sought to bring home to his hearers the deadening, blunting effects of sin; Israel's tragic ignorance concerning their spiritual state, and that this ignorance resulted from a lack of knowledge of God. Ignoring Him, and departing from His word, Israel became deluded and self-deceived. "Aliens devour his strength," the prophet declared, "and he knows it not: gray hairs are sprinkled upon him, and he knows it not" (7:9). How vividly this comment recalls the story of Samson! Yet, knowing that story, the people of Israel behaved exactly as Samson did, in self-indulgence and sinful dallying with the enemies of God. And so do we!

It was Amos, Hosea's immediate predecessor, who—probably a few years before Hosea uttered his prophecies—asked the rhetorical question, "Can two walk together, except they be agreed?" He implied that Israel could walk with God only when obedient to His will. The same thought underlies Hosea's impassioned utterances. To court the patronage of "strangers"—Gentile and pagan nations—was to affront the covenant God of Israel; and it miserably failed to bring satisfaction or security. On the contrary, it sapped their resources and undermined the foundations of national stability. And all the while Israel failed to realise what was happening. Strength diminished, without their knowing it; the evidences of declining powers went un-noticed.

It is a graphic picture of the backslider. Loss of spiritual vitality, through involvement in worldly affairs, neglect of the means of grace in personal walk with the Lord, is seldom dramatic: rather, it is so gradual as to be practically unrecognised—and especially so by the one concerned; often other people discern the condition sooner than the man or woman grown lukewarm in love to the Lord. The supreme tragedy is that, even when confronted with the facts, and at last aware of the tokens of deterioration, the backslider is often by now so far departed from the Lord as to be unconcerned, numbed in conscience, regardless of the eternal consequences of his condition: "they do not return to the Lord their God," says Hosea, "nor seek Him, for all this" (7:10).

This leads on to the fourth of Hosea's series of metaphors—"Ephraim is like a dove, silly and without sense; calling to Egypt, going to Assyria" (7:11). What more eloquent figure of speech could any prophet find for the backslider and "ditherer"—the one who knows the truth but doesn't do it—be it nation or individual, than this? As Israel wavered in opinion whether to turn to Egypt or Assyria for deliverance, so the Christian who looks to the world rather than to the Lord finds himself a mere shuttlecock between conflicting passions and policies.

Turning from God is ever the ultimate folly, for it means forsaking the Rock of our salvation for the storms and fierce currents of swirling seas of evil. A silly dove, leaving the "ark" of covenant relationship with God, for the dangers and disasters of flirting with worldly enticements. A silly dove "without a heart" (*AV*) indeed —or, as perhaps the term should be interpreted, "without understanding" of spiritual verities and values.

No wonder the chapter ends upon a most solemn note—the pronouncement of the judgment long impending: "Woe unto them, for they have fled from me! Destruction to them, for they have rebelled against me" (7:13). Despite warning and clearest intimation of the consequences of their evil ways, "they do not cry to me from the heart," says God; "I would redeem them, but they speak lies against me." They make profession of penitence, but it is not true repentance: "they return, but not to the Most High" (7:16); rather, as *RSV* renders this phrase, "They turn to Baal." Their semblance of piety is hypocritical; they are a "deceitful bow," shooting wide of the mark, falling far short of true loyalty to the Lord.

No wonder their doom was sealed. Hosea anticipates the declaration of the apostle, that "the wages of sin is death." Doubtless he would also have gone on gladly to proclaim, if he had been able to anticipate the glorious tidings of the new covenant, "but the gift of God is eternal life through Jesus Christ our Lord."

9

Reaping the Whirlwind

It was a heart-breaking task that the minor prophets had to fulfil, in pleading with an unrepentant, unresponsive people; and to this was added the stern responsibility of pronouncing judgment upon them—their own kinsfolk and nation. In every case, however, before judgment was pronounced repeated warning was given, and protracted opportunity to turn from evil ways to the Lord.

Once again, therefore, Hosea sounded the alarm (8:1). "Set the trumpet to thy mouth," the Lord had commanded; the assailant would come "as an eagle"—or, more correctly, "as a vulture" (*RSV*). This is an apt description of Assyria, both in its swift swoop upon its victims, and in its pitiless tearing asunder of the prey. The most cruel of the ancient empire-states, Assyria boasted in its monuments—many extant today in the British Museum—of its brutalities toward the people it conquered. This terrible foe would assail "the house of the Lord"—His covenant people; and He would allow it: indeed, He would use Assyria as the rod of His chastisement, "because they have transgressed my covenant, and trespassed against my law." By their disobedience and self-will Israel had been unfaithful in relationship to the Lord; by violating His law they had rejected His word and refused obedience to His will. It was to a people ripe for judgment that this stern oracle was spoken.

In the hour of calamity, "Israel shall cry unto me, My God, we know Thee" (8:2). Alas, that claim upon His compassion would be uttered too late, the prophet foretold; the day of grace would, for them, have ended. As in the case of the unwise virgins who found themselves without oil in their lamps when the bridegroom came, the door would be closed against them, and the solemn disavowal declared, "I know you not."

There is, on the part of many people, religious and otherwise, an assumption that they can turn to God whenever they will, and lay claim upon His mercy; they seem to think that He will be flattered by their attentions, even though these be but a blunt demand for help in time of desperate need, or for deliverance from calamity brought upon them by defiance of His revealed will. Now it is true that the compassions of God are past our understanding; that in numberless cases He *does* hear such cries of distress, so that the most unworthy, turning to Him in desperation, find grace to help in time of need. That is both the character and the characteristic of our God, in this day of grace. But we cannot affirm too emphatically—as the prophets repeatedly insisted—that this will not be so in the long-anticipated "day of the Lord." Then, when His judgments are in operation, it will be too late to seek His favour. The day of grace will have run its course. It will be vain to appeal to the Lord against His own judgments; unavailing to plead for mercy after its final rejection. We need to stress to our own apostate generation with all the powers at our command, "Today if ye will hear His voice, harden not your hearts . . ." "Behold, now is the accepted time; behold, now is the day of salvation" (Heb. 3:15; 2 Cor. 6:2).

What, then, called forth this judgment against Israel, and sealed their doom? The answer is clear enough, and has been given repeatedly by Hosea. Nevertheless the prophet once more sets forth the divine indictment, "that every mouth may be stopped": it is, "Israel has spurned the good" (8:3). In this abrupt sentence the prophet sums up the sin of Israel: rejection of God, refusal to hear and heed His word, with consequent departure from His will and way. He then proceeds to specific charges, which illustrate the major indictment: "They have set up kings, but not by me: they have made princes, and I knew it not: of their silver and their gold they have made them idols . . ." (8:4). They had, in a word, left God out of account in the ordering of their lives and the conduct of their affairs. They had behaved as if He didn't exist; as if He were not the Lord their God. Indeed, from the very gifts He had bestowed upon them, they made idols. The astounding folly of it! People who knew the living God, Maker of heaven and earth; who had been called into covenant relationship with Him, and had the glorious heritage of His grace and bounty to their fathers and to themselves, yet made idols—the product of their own imagination and the work of their own hands—and worshipped them, rather than the true and only Lord God Almighty. No wonder God declared, in words of withering scorn, "I have spurned your calf, O Samaria. Mine anger burns against them" (8 : 5). Their spurning of "good" resulted in His spurning of them and their idols.

Possibly the "calf"—or more probably, bull—worshipped in Samaria had been intended originally as an aid to the worship of Jehovah, as was the calf made by Aaron when Moses was in the mount (Exod. 32:4). It has never been an easy matter to maintain worship of the unseen God, in spirit and in truth; fallen man longs for a visible object of worship. Therein lies the appeal of idolatry, and the great danger of all objective "aids to devotion." While ostensibly the "calf," both of the Israelites in the wilderness and of Ephraim in Samaria, might have been intended at first as a means of focusing thought and devotion upon the worship of Jehovah, it soon became a mere idol, an object of worship in itself. It was so, too, with the ephod which Gideon made, with the intention that it should stimulate and encourage the worship of Jehovah; but instead, "all Israel went a-whoring after it: which thing became a snare unto Gideon and to his house" (Judges 8:27).

Is not the lesson clear and plain in this Christian era also? While crucifixes and images are allegedly a means of focusing faith and prayer, one has only to visit certain churches to realise that they have become, in fact, idols. The commandment remains unrevoked: "Thou shalt not make unto thee any graven image, or any likeness of any thing that is in heaven above, or any thing that is in the earth beneath . . ." (Exod. 20:4).

As if to spell out this simple statement concerning Ephraim's sinful idolatry and its consequences, Hosea goes on to assert, "the workman made it; therefore it is not God: but the calf of Samaria shall be broken in pieces" (8:6). Then he utters a phrase which has become proverbial among many nations and in many languages: "They have sown the wind, and they shall reap the whirlwind" (8:7). They have given their energies of mind and heart, their spiritual and physical strength, to the "sowing" of what cannot possibly produce a "harvest" for their spiritual good; they have devoted their time and resources to matters which can bring no benefit, in terms of eternal well-being. Instead, what they have favoured and fostered will turn out to be a devastating force of evil; a whirlwind which will destroy and scatter all they hoped to gain. The utter folly of their behaviour, the futility of their hopes for pleasure and prosperity in the ways of ungodliness is underlined: "it hath no stalk"—no possibility or promise even, of fruitfulness.

From metaphor, Hosea passes to plainest prediction: "Israel is swallowed up: now shall they be among the Gentiles . . . for they are gone up to Assyria." And the reason: "Ephraim hath hired lovers" (8:9). Israel was apostate; Jehovah's Gomer, His adulterous wife. Regardless of God, they looked entirely to their heathen neighbours for help and deliverance. But "though they hire allies among the nations I will soon gather them up" (8 : 10), *i.e.*, send them into exile.

In all this, the people of Israel were not irreligious. Indeed, they had "multiplied altars" (8:11), but not for the worship of God; rather, Hosea says they were "for sinning." Much of the idolatrous cult-worship was attended by degraded rites; but the prophet's denunciation is not confined to these. His condemnation embraces all forms of worship outside that ordained by God; all that was not according to His command and submissive to His will.

It is arresting that *religion* apart from revelation is regarded in the Scriptures as a foremost foe of God and of His people. It was not agnosticism but false religion which became a snare to Israel even on their journey from Egypt to the promised land; and it remained so ever after. And even more insidious than palpably false religion was the degradation of the true faith into a lifeless formalism and meaningless observance of ceremonies. This deadened the conscience, numbed the spirit, and lifted up the proud heart of man. It was the religious authorities of His day who would have nothing to do with Jesus, and plotted and planned His death. It was priests and pundits of the law who crucified the Lord of glory.

This is a pertinent topic for today, when the popular view is that any religion is better than none; and that there are elements of truth in all religions, so that we can and should learn from one another, and meet together on a common basis of nebulous religious belief. This "broad-minded" ecumenical outlook emphasises certain emotive matters, such as the love of God and our Lord's desire for unity among His people, but strictly avoids the major issues of Biblical faith and practice. Religion is put firmly before conviction; outward appearance before the reality of inward faith. Human organisation and religious activity seem to be far more prominent than the worship of Almighty God in spirit and in truth. There is a danger, at least, of erecting "altars for sinning." "They love sacrifice . . . but the Lord has no delight in them" (8:13).

This chapter 8, indeed, is one of almost unrelieved severity. "Now will He remember their iniquity, and punish their sins" (8:13); they shall "return unto Egypt"—*i.e.*, go again into captivity

—"For Israel hath forgotten his Maker . . . but I will send a fire upon his cities, and it shall devour the palaces thereof" (8:14). But that is not God's last word to Israel. Hosea had happier tidings in store.

10

Days of Recompense

WHEN the sun is shining serenely from a clear heaven, it is difficult to believe that soon thunder-clouds will darken the horizon, spread rapidly across the sky, and then break in a violent, devastating storm. It was equally difficult for the Israelites to believe, in times of prosperity, the warnings of the prophets concerning impending judgment; just as today the message of our Lord's Second Advent—when, all too infrequently, it is mentioned—falls largely upon incredulous ears. The attitude of the majority of people was well foretold by Peter: "There shall come in the last days scoffers . . . saying, Where is the promise of His coming? for since the fathers fell asleep, all things continue as they were from the beginning of creation . . ." (2 Pet. 3:3–4). People are incredibly self-deceived, when things are going well, that the "never-had-it-so-good" conditions will not only persist, but get better and better. Any suggestion of possible disaster ahead is rejected wrathfully. Recollection of past bitter experiences is deliberately wiped from memory, and life is ordered as if the present felicity will flourish for ever. So it is in Britain today; and so it was in Israel of oid.

It is no wonder, then, that Hosea and his ministry were resented and rejected. Yet, as the "watchman of Ephraim" (9:8) he could not but tell forth all that the Lord constrained him to utter. The people of Israel could never say they had not been explicitly warned of judgment to come, and earnestly entreated to repent in time to ensure the repeal of their predicted doom. After stating clearly not only that Israel would be conquered and carried away into captivity by Assyria, Hosea goes on to foretell graphically, in chapter 9, the conditions which the faithless people of God would experience in their expulsion from their land and exile among foreigners.

First, however, he compassionately exhorts them not to continue in their self-deception regarding their immediate, short-lived prosperity. "Rejoice not, O Israel. Exult not like the peoples . . ."—that is, in the good harvest they had gathered; for like their idolatrous neighbours they had attributed this bounty, not to God, the true

Giver of all, but to Baal, the fertility god: "for you have played the harlot, forsaking your God. You have loved a harlot's hire upon all threshing floors" (9:1). This oracle, like those of Amos, was evidently delivered during the autumn "harvest festival." In the very act of gathering and threshing the abundant yield of their fields, they gave thanks and presented offerings to Baal. Therefore God would take from them the gifts they had ungratefully and sinfully attributed to the deities and evil rites of the pagan peoples around them.

And so they sealed their doom: "They shall not remain in the land of the Lord; but Ephraim . . . shall eat unclean food in Assyria" (9:3). Then Hosea goes on graphically to describe their desperate plight when God's back would be turned upon them, and the means of grace withdrawn. Over and above the temporal distress of defeat and exile, of expulsion from their homes and homeland, of the loss of everything they possessed and valued, would be the inability to turn to the Lord or to call upon His mercy. The very bread they would eat—the miserable fare permitted by the conquerors—would be unclean, because unconsecrated by the offering of the firstfruits to God; nor would there be any possibility of propitiation of the Almighty through sacrifice (9:4). Their "days of visitation" would have come; the "days of recompense" in which they would reap the full and unrelieved penalty of their wilful apostasy. They would be cast off by the One whom they had, in their arrogant folly, ignored and defied.

How severe a task was that of Hosea, in delivering such a message, knowing that it would soon come to pass, although the people jeered at him for saying so! "The prophet is a fool," they said—as the rebellious in every generation have declared concerning the Lord's spokesmen. But like Jeremiah, every servant of God to whom His word comes, cannot but speak forth that word: it is as a fire in the bones, a compulsion of the Spirit which cannot be gainsaid. God has never yet left Himself without a witness; and He never will.

In a poignant passage, Hosea contrasts the early responsiveness of Israel to the love and covenant grace of God, with their present hardness of heart—"I found Israel like grapes in the wilderness," God said; "I saw your fathers as the first-ripe in the fig tree" (9:10). What rejoicing to the heart of a weary traveller is the sight in the desert of a beautiful oasis, where luscious grapes and first-ripe figs seem so much more delightsome than in any other setting or circumstances. So the "first love" of Israel for the Lord, in the wilderness of Sinai, was to Him the supreme occasion of rejoicing in His people. Alas, they soon lost the glow of that first love, and brought grief to His heart, instead of gratification: they "went to Baal-peor" —their first, portentous succumbing to the lure of Baal (9 : 10).

The story of that ancient sin is well known: how God protected His people against the schemings of Balak, and obliged Balaam, the mercenary prophet, to bless instead of cursing them; yet, despite that wondrous deliverance, and reversal of the purposes of their adversaries, Israel allowed themselves to be ensnared by Balaam into sexual indulgence (Num. 25 : 3). That was the first fatal contact with what proved to be their most insidious temptation and their besetting sin. From that time they were seldom free of it. How it behoves us to learn the lesson and heed the warning to beware of the beginnings of sin. To yield to temptation is to step out upon a slippery slope from which it is most difficult to escape.

From that initial transgression Israel had so far progressed in evil that "they have deeply corrupted themselves, as in the days of Gibeah" (9 : 9). Therefore "He will remember their iniquity, He will visit their sins . . ." and in consequence "their glory shall fly away like a bird" (9 : 11). In stern and terrible words Hosea describes the agony which would characterise the conquest by Assyria, when women would cry for "a miscarrying womb and dry breasts," because "Ephraim shall bring forth children to the murderer" (9 : 13–14). These chilling words are an old covenant anticipation of the solemn adjuration of our Lord to the daughters of Jerusalem, "Weep not for me, but weep for yourselves and your children. For behold, the days are coming in which they shall say, Blessed are the barren, and the wombs that never bare, and the paps which never gave suck. Then shall they begin to say to the mountains, Fall on us; and to the hills, Cover us. For if they do these things in a green tree, what shall be done in the dry?" (Luke 23 : 28–31).

And so the final sentence is pronounced: "Ephraim is smitten . . . my God will cast them away because they did not hearken unto Him: and they shall be wanderers among the nations" (9 : 16–17). How strikingly that prediction has been fulfilled: the "lost ten tribes" have indeed been, ever since, "wanderers among the nations." The word of God has been in this, as in all its predictions regarding Israel, literally fulfilled: it is utterly reliable, the inspired, authentic word of God to all mankind.

11

An Empty Vine

As the rose is the national emblem of England, the thistle of Scotland, and shamrock of Ireland, so the vine was the emblem of Israel (Psa. 80 : 8–14; Isa. 5 : 1–5, etc). It would seem also that the fig-tree was regarded as symbolic of the nation: at least, our Lord's parable concerning it might carry that implication (Luke 21 : 29–33); and there is a hint of this also in the story of the cursing of the barren fig-tree—though perhaps these refer more particularly to the city of Jerusalem than to the nation of Israel in general. But the vine was pre-eminently the national symbol, and no fewer than five of our Lord's parables use it in this way. It is profoundly significant, of course, that Jesus, in describing Himself as the true vine and His disciples as the branches, transferred the imagery from Israel to the church.

It is therefore a graphic metaphor which, according to the *AV*, Hosea uses when he declares that "Israel is an empty vine" (10 : 1). This arresting simile depicts the utter failure of the nation to produce "fruit unto righteousness"; to bring forth that which gratifies and glorifies God. It expresses in a terse phrase the entire content of Isaiah's parable of the vineyard (Isa. 5). Unfortunately for this long-held interpretation, however, this rendering of the verse in the *AV* is not valid: what Hosea wrote is more correctly translated by the *RSV*, "Israel is a luxuriant vine . . ." The charge of the prophet was that Israel, greatly blessed by God, were not giving Him the gratitude and worship which were His due, but rather were *emptying out* their wealth—lavishing their thanksgivings and their gifts—upon false gods. From the very bounty received from Jehovah, they were making sacrifices and offerings to Baal. "The more his (Israel's) fruit increased the more altars he built . . ." But the time of reckoning had come. "Now they must bear their guilt. The Lord will break down their altars and destroy their pillars"—that is, their idolatrous groves (10 : 2).

In dramatic words the prophet depicts the utterly lawless attitude of the people toward both God and their king—"We fear not the

Lord; and a king, what could he do for us?" Again Ellison gives this a new twist, however, in his rendering, ". . . they say, No king for us! For we do not fear the Lord, and what could the king do for us?" He adds that the oracle "must come from the last desperate days of Israel after the murder of Pekah." In such conditions, justice collapsed and injustice abounded. Therefore "judgment springs up like poisonous weeds in the furrows of the field"—a figure of speech which would be much more meaningful to an agricultural people than it is to urban readers today. Even so, no one who has seen a promising crop ruined by fast-growing weeds which swamp and stifle it, can miss the pungency of Hosea's prediction. The land was ripe for *God's* judgment!

Once more the prophet demonstrates the futility of idol worship, as he describes the consternation of the people of Samaria when their idol is captured and borne away as a spoil of war. They "tremble for the calf of Beth-aven." Well might both its worshippers and its priests wail over it, for "the thing itself"—note the scorn of the description—"is carried to Assyria" (10 : 5–6). That is a true picture of the ultimate tragedy of all idolatry: its total inability to help in time of need, and its final exposure as vain and foolish and futile. The gods of today—the idols of our materialistic generation; the things we set our hearts on, and value above all else, although they are but the works of men's hands—these will in the end prove as unavailing to deliver or to comfort in the day of calamity as was the calf of Beth-aven. Thorns and thistles—tokens of the curse ensuing upon the sin of Adam—will come up on the idolatrous altars, Hosea affirmed, bearing evidence to all who might behold that God had visited in judgment the adulterous Israelites who worshipped there, and blighted both the place and the object of their idolatrous rites.

Once more Hosea recalls an ancient sin—that committed at Gibeah, notorious for the shameful outrage by Benjamites which shocked the nation: but the prophet declares that the selfsame sin had persisted through all the intervening generations, and Israel still stood upon that same ground. But there, at long last, condign punishment would overtake them: "they are chastised for their double iniquity"—that of the past and of the present; or maybe, for their double sin of rejection of God and worship of idols (10 : 9–10).

Then the mood of the prophet, and of his prophecy, changes. Into the stern message of judgment a wooing note irrupts. God is love, and in wrath He ever remembers mercy. Ephraim is depicted as a "trained heifer that loveth to thresh" (10 : 11); a domestic pet, indulged and even pampered: "and I spared her fair neck," says the Lord. Instead of submitting her to a harsh yoke, God had so greatly blessed Israel that she had but the lightest of duties; pleasant occupation and abundant rewards. It is a picture of the material prosperity with which God had endowed His people in the "land flowing with milk and honey." But that state of affairs was to end. They had abused His bounty, desiring only an easy life and unlimited indulgences. They prized His gifts but scorned the Giver. Accordingly "I will put Ephraim to the yoke." A burdensome bondage would be their lot.

Yet even as he tells of it, Hosea pleads with the people to repent. "Sow for yourselves righteousness . . ." he urges; "break up your fallow ground" (10 : 12). It was not too late, even at that eleventh hour, to seek the Lord; if only they would do so, He would "come and rain salvation" upon them. Oh, the longsuffering and lovingkindness of our God! His chastisements are designed for His children's good; and until the crack of doom He pleads with them to turn from their wicked ways and beseech His pardoning grace.

Alas, Israel never learned the lesson of their own experience, or heeded the counsels of the Lord's messengers. "Ye have ploughed wickedness, ye have reaped iniquity; ye have eaten the fruit of lies" (10 : 13). Because they trusted in their own wisdom and were determined to go their own way, in defiance of God's word and will, "therefore the tumult of war shall arise among your people, and all your fortresses shall be destroyed" (10 : 14). There is no alternative to judgment for those who persist in rejecting the way of escape.

12

Cords of Compassion

It is characteristic of Hosea that—truly reflecting the mind and heart of God—he alternates in his message between the stern note of warning of impending judgment and tender expression of compassion and appeal. In this, of course, he infuses into his prophetic ministry the conflicting emotions of his personal experience with Gomer. In the latter part of his book the winsome note predominates, although God's judgment on sin is never cancelled or moderated except upon the grounds of true repentance and seeking of His grace.

In that fact lay the burden of the prophets—and, if we may reverently say so, the problem of the Lord. God is love; He delights in mercy, and longs to forgive and restore His wayward people—His adulterous wife. He never, however, can condone sin; never overlook iniquity. His character as the high and holy one cannot ignore the fact of defilement; cannot tolerate rebellion and resentment. Judgment on sin is essential and inevitable; yet judgment is the most distressful of His acts. There is pain in the proclamation of it, and in the voice of the prophet who utters it.

These mingled notes are exemplified in Hosea 11. In all Scripture there is no more tender portrayal of God's love for His chosen people, than the picture of Israel as "a child" called out of Egypt —"I taught Ephraim to walk, I took them up in my arms . . ." (11 : 1, 3). Hosea often harks back to the early days of the nation's history, both in their "first love" and also in their early self-will and apostasy. If God recalls Baal-peor and the sin of Gibeah, He also remembers the time when Israel was "like grapes in the wilderness . . . like the first fruit of the fig tree in its first season" (9 : 10).

Here the recollection is particularly pleasing: Israel is likened to a young child, with implicit trust in and unsullied love for the one who cares for him. The word-picture is especially vivid: as a parent teaches a child to walk, holding him under the arms, and encouraging him in his first steps, so God had cared for and delighted in His people. Yet, so soon, "the more I called them"—through the prophets—"the more they went from me; they kept sacrificing to the Baals, and burning incense to idols" (11 : 2). Perhaps here, in these two verses, we discern as clearly as anywhere in this book, what the coldness of heart of His people means to God; what sorrow it brings to Him, and deprivation of the joy He should have in them. As the distress of a parent over a wayward son is commensurate with his love for that son, so the sorrow of God over sinful Israel is commensurate with that love which "passeth all understanding."

From very infancy, as it were, Israel had been for the most part unthankful and unresponding. Despite all the manifest grace and bounty of God, they seemed oblivious of their privilege as His covenant people: they "did not know that I healed them"—that is, kept them in health and safety. It was God who guided and protected them through all the hazards of their wilderness journeying; who led them into the promised land and gave it into their possession. "I led them with cords of compassion, and with bands of love" (11 : 4); moreover, the Lord smoothed their way before them, and gave them victory over their enemies—"I became to them as one who eases the yoke on their jaws, and I bent down to them and fed them." Is there a hint in this reminder of past mercies that He, the unchanging Lord, will be equally ready to "ease the yoke" of Assyrian bondage foretold as coming upon them as His judgment (10 : 11) if only they will turn to Him and call for mercy?

Alas, there was no sign of such turning; and so they should "return to Egypt"—to captivity similar to that from which their fathers were delivered, but in their case Assyria would take the place of Egypt (11 : 5). "My people are bent on turning away from me; so they are appointed to the yoke, and none shall remove it" (11 : 7).

The pendulum having swung from compassion to severity, returned again to a note of yearning more poignant than ever before; and in one of the most moving passages of the book the Lord says through Hosea—

How can I give you up, O Ephraim!
  How can I hand you over, O Israel!
How can I make you like Admah!
  How can I treat you like Zeboim!
My heart recoils within me,
  My compassions grow warm and tender (11 : 8).

Here, as in many Scriptures, the language is anthropomorphic—as if God were subject to our human emotions and reactions to situations. How shall the thoughts of God—which are high above ours as the heavens are high above the earth—be conveyed except in terms of our human feelings and experiences; how shall we understand unless they are expressed and interpreted in language related to our own emotions? God is not swayed by moods nor affected by varying feelings; yet in His love He grieves over the waywardness of His people and longs for their well-being. If Jesus was "moved with compassion" over the multitudes, no less is God compassionate and tender in His unfailing love toward an unworthy race. He just *cannot* "hand over" Israel to ultimate and final judgment; cannot destroy them as He destroyed the cities of the plain.

> I will not execute my fierce anger,
> I will not again destroy Ephraim;
> for I am God and not man,
> the Holy One in your midst,
> and I will not come to destroy.

That seems like a rescinding of the sentence pronounced upon Israel; but Hosea goes on immediately to make clear that the assault by Assyria and the captivity of Ephraim, are not revoked. Sin must bear its penalty; spiritual adultery must be punished. But *beyond* the conquest and the scattering would ensue a regathering—"they shall come trembling like birds from Egypt, and like doves from the land of Assyria; and I will return them to their homes, says the Lord" (11 : 11).

Hosea joins with other prophets in foreseeing and foretelling that great and final "day of the Lord" when His purposes in and for and through Israel shall ultimately be realised. No matter how unfaithful they may be, God is "not a man" that *He* should be unfaithful to His covenant, or that He should fail in the realisation of His purposes. Israel shall yet turn to Him with all their hearts; shall recognise and welcome their Messiah, and "a nation shall be born in a day." Foregleams of that "great light" break upon the horizon in this chapter; they shine with clearer and more brilliant rays as Hosea's prophecy moves to its climax.

13

False Balances

WHILE spiritual adultery was Hosea's main indictment against Israel, there were other matters of failure in everyday conduct which contributed to their guilt, and concerning some of these the prophet makes more mundane charges in chapter 12. Here Judah also is arraigned before the bar of the divine judgment, together with Israel, more specifically than before: hitherto there have been only prophetic asides addressed to the southern kingdom. The two peoples are coupled together, and contrasted, in 11 : 12—which is, in the Hebrew text, the beginning of chapter 12—"Ephraim has compassed me with lies, and the house of Israel with deceit; but Judah is still known by God, and is faithful to the Holy One." Lest Judah should preen herself upon this distinction between two kingdoms, however, the prophet goes on to show that this "faithfulness" was a comparative matter only. "The Lord has an indictment against Judah, and will punish Jacob according to his ways, and requite him according to his deeds . . ." (12 : 2). It is as if God were emphasising, through the prophet, that He has no favourites. The flagrant sin of Israel was about to receive its long-merited judgment; but while thus engaged with the northern kingdom, the Lord would not turn a "blind eye" to Judah. It sometimes seems that some evil-doers "get away with it" while others suffer: but that is never true in the long term of God's dealings with men. God never condones in one what He condemns in another. He is a God of absolute righteousness and justice, and He preserves a perfect balance in all His dealings—as will ultimately be manifest at the great white throne.

Yet again Hosea finds permanent characteristics of the national life indicated from their earliest days; indeed, from the very birth of Jacob, when he revealed the acquisitive propensity which proved to be his undoing, by grasping his brother's heel as he left the womb (12 : 3). But Jacob, crafty and greedy though he was, yet had a keen sense of the supreme value of spiritual verities; he had a reverential awe of God, and a desire to worship and honour Him. And so, with all his failings, he "strove with the angel and prevailed," and was led through varied experiences to Bethel, where God "spoke with him" (12 : 4). His descendants are therefore exhorted to learn from their progenitor, and despite their faults and failings, to "turn to the Lord thy God: keep mercy and judgment, and wait on thy God continually" (v. 6). That is the insistent note in all the prophetic oracles, repeated here most clearly.

This admonishment of Judah comes as an interlude in the arraignment of Israel. The northern kingdom's foreign policy, of attempting to appease both Assyria and Egypt, instead of trusting in God, is once more condemned: "Ephraim herds (shepherds) the wind . . . they make a bargain with Assyria, and oil is carried to Egypt" (12 : 1). This correct rendering of the *RSV* is much more vivid than "Ephraim feedeth on wind" (*AV*). There is a richness of significance in the word "shepherd" which would mean more to the Israelites of Hosea's day than to Western city-dwellers of this twentieth century; but even we can appreciate the care and concern it connotes: the devoted solicitude of the shepherd for his sheep. And *this* had been lavished by foolish Israel upon—wind: they had given thought and effort and money and even worship to idols that would profit them nothing. It was vain and utterly foolish. They also had adopted policies which would bring them no good, but rather would ruin them. The double-dealing of their relationships with the two great rival powers would recoil upon them: they would "shepherd" nothing but a devastating tornado.

From foreign policy, Hosea turns to matters of conduct in everyday life. Ephraim is "a trader, in whose hands are false balances; he loves to oppress . . ." (12 : 7). In this verse there is a most interesting play upon words which is lost in our English versions. The word rendered "merchantman" (*AV*) or "trader" (*RSV*) is literally, "Canaanite." The Phoenicians were renowned as merchants: it came about, therefore, that the word "Canaanite" became a technical term for a trader. They were notoriously not too scrupulous, and so the word has also undertones of sharp practice, as well as trading. That is the sting of Hosea's allegation. Ephraim had adopted not only Canaanite methods but also Canaanite standards and subterfuges. Here is an OT example of conformity to the world, against which we are so repeatedly warned in the NT. Of course, we have to live in the world, and engage in its business and affairs; but the danger for the man of God lies in conforming to the world's ways and being degraded to its levels of conduct.

Ephraim has said, "Ah, but I am rich,
I have gained wealth for myself";
but all his riches can never offset
the guilt he has incurred (v. 8).

This rendering of the *RSV*, however, obscures a most important factor in the situation, expressed clearly in both the *AV* and *RV*—that Israel made vigorous self-defence of its attitude and conduct: "Ephraim said, Yet I am become rich, and have found me out substance: in all my labours they shall find none iniquity in me that were sin" (*AV*). This rendering has strong support from the commentators. Ellicott says: "Translate, *And Ephraim saith, Surely I have become wealthy; I have gotten me substance* (*i.e.*, by legitimate means, not robbery): *all my earnings bring me not guilt as would be sin.*" The IVF *New Bible Commentary* observes: "Israel has a false basis of self-defence: he points to the riches he has acquired as a sure sign of God's favour to him." And *The Wycliffe Bible Commentary*: "Living like her Canaanite neighbours, Israel had become proud and arrogant. She did not even realise that her life had become marked by sin."

It is characteristic of the deceitfulness of sin, that it numbs the conscience and beguiles the sinner into believing that he is not at fault. One can almost hear the supercilious retort of the merchantman to the prophet, concerning some shady transaction, "There's nothing wrong with that!" Doubtless those who, in the days of our Lord, pursued their business in the temple, debasing it into "an house of merchandise," put forward the self-same plea.

This soporific to conscience is still in regular use—and alas, all too effectually! It was so in Laodicea: "Thou sayest, I am rich, and increased with goods, and have need of nothing; and knowest not that thou are wretched, and miserable, and poor, and blind, and naked . . ." It is so easy to adopt the standards of the world, to absorb the spirit of the age, and become conformed to its ways. The Christian's standard, however, his guide and safeguard, should be the word of God (Hosea 12 : 10). "I counsel thee," said the ascended Lord to the Laodiceans, "to buy of me gold tried in the fire, that thou mayest be rich; and white raiment that thou mayest be clothed, and that the shame of thy nakedness do not appear; and anoint thine eyes with eyesalve, that thou mayest see. . . ."

Israel, however, was heedless of every warning and unresponsive to every exhortation. Therefore God, who brought their fathers out of Egypt, would send them back again into captivity; they should be banished from their houses, and should again dwell in tents, as during the wilderness wanderings—a people rootless, without home or possessions: for in forsaking God, and violating His law, they forfeited all that they so proudly thought they owned, but in fact had received solely from His good hand (12 : 9).

In vindication of the true justice of His sentence against them, the Lord reminds Israel that He had warned and exhorted them through prophets, and revealed His will by means of visions and parables (12: 10). Then, in an arresting interrogation, He demands, "Is there iniquity in Gilead?" (12: 11). This *AV* rendering brings to mind again the complementary question in Jeremiah, "Is there no balm in Gilead?" (Jer. 8: 22). It would seem that this was a proverbial saying: the resin derived from trees in Gilead was renowned for its healing qualities. It became symbolic of the healing ministry of the Lord's messengers—the restoring of the people to spiritual health and right relationship to God, through heeding the words of the prophets. But that ministry, rejected, became a pronouncing of punishment: the altars of their idols would be overthrown in the furrows of their fields (12: 11).

Once more a gleam of light breaks through the gloom of Hosea's prediction. Again glancing back over the nation's history, the prophet recalls how Jacob "served for a wife" in Syria, but in due course returned to the land of promise. Similarly Jacob's descendants had endured servitude in Egypt, but God delivered them and brought them into the land of their possession. So also would He bring back a remnant from this impending expulsion and captivity: but this is implied rather than explicitly stated in these verses, though gloriously proclaimed in the two following chapters. Here, chapter 12 ends with stern reminder that they are about to reap what they have sown; that divine judgment is consequent upon repeated and unrepented sin. Those sombre hues, however, are the intensification of darkness before the dawn!

14

Final Diagnosis and Doom

CONDITIONS of life today are so different from those in ancient Israel that, try as we might, it is impossible to put ourselves in the shoes of the prophets, and recapture their emotions as they delivered their inspired utterances. Nevertheless it needs no great effort to enter in measure into their turbulent feelings of alternating hope and despair, as their warnings were disregarded and exhortations to repentance rejected.

Hosea had poured out his heart in entreaty to a people over whom he yearned as earnestly as, in personal unfaltering love, he yearned over his adulterous wife, Gomer. Now, every effort of God Himself, and of His spokesman, having proved unavailing to quicken the stony heart of Ephraim, the prophet in a short, moving passage (13: 1–12) makes his final diagnosis of the nation's condition, and pronounces its doom. Divine love has run its full course in an effort to redeem and restore "harlot" Israel; now the prophet sorrowfully recognises that they are irrevocably settled in their sinful ways, and there is no hope of their repenting.

Like some other passages in the prophets, this most movingly expresses the travail of the heart of God at the determined apostasy of His people; His reluctance to give them up, and to bring upon them the judgment they so richly deserve. Once more the prophet portrays, in vivid, kaleidoscopic terms, what they *were*, in contrast with what they *might have been*. "When Ephraim spake trembling, he exalted himself in Israel; but when he offended in Baal, he died" (13: 1). This *AV* rendering is attractive, in its suggestion that humility was the secret of Ephraim's strength; but it is misleading, for the *RSV* correctly translates the verse—

> When Ephraim spoke, men trembled;
> he exalted himself in Israel;
> but when he incurred guilt through Baal he died.

There was a time when Ephraim reached the peak of power and prestige, under the good hand of God, in the heyday of the united tribes of Israel. These former cringing slaves of Pharaoh had been brought to a condition of authority and strength; and all they were, all they possessed, they owed to God. But all too soon they turned away from Him; and in succumbing to the lure of Baalim, they *died*. That is the stark fact of the consequence of sin. We are apt to regard the warning to Adam, "in the day that thou eatest thereof thou shalt surely die," as metaphorical; and its NT counterpart, "the wages of sin is death" as relating solely to the future state. Sin brings death, however: immediate, here and now. Sin separates from God; it makes the sinner deaf to His voice, insensible to His constraints—in effect, spiritually dead.

Christian people are too much like Ephraim, in reluctance to face up to the facts concerning sin: but this is its character, and this is its consequence. Sin indulged in any life, brings *death*—not mere estrangement from God, a cooling-off of love to Him, but spiritual death. This is evinced by the silencing of conscience, the quenching of prayer, neglect of the means of grace, and finally, loss of all sense of relationship to God. Sin is the most insidious spiritual disease, fatal in its effects: we can never regard it too seriously or shun it too earnestly.

The ultimate consequence of Israel's chosen course, now about to reach its full realisation, had in fact been operative ever since they deliberately turned from Jehovah and transferred their loyalty to Baal. The evidence of this—the full justification for their condemnation by God—is cited in 13 : 2,

> . . . they sin more and more,
>   and make for themselves molten images,
> idols skilfully made of their silver,
>   all of them work of their craftsmen.
> Sacrifice to these, they say.
>   Men kiss calves!

In a brief moment of conviction and superficial concern, Israel had professed repentance; but God knew that their "goodness" was but "a morning cloud; and as the early dew it goeth away." Now those same figures of speech are used concerning the dispersing of Israel from their homeland—

> Therefore shall they be like the morning mist
>   or like the dew that goes early away . . . (13 : 3)

No fewer than four metaphors are used in this verse, to illustrate the finality of the Lord's scattering of Ephraim—the morning mist, the dew, chaff that swirls from the threshing floor, and smoke dispersing through a window. There is irony in the use of these, as if the Lord would say that, since their repentance had been superficial, their judgment would be in keeping; if their sorrow for sin had been insubstantial, so would they themselves be in their decimation and humiliating subjugation by Assyria. As they had dealt with God, so would He deal with them.

All this is presented by the prophet against the background of their privileged relationship to God, and long experience of His grace. He had redeemed them from Egypt, and had oft demonstrated that "beside me there is no Saviour" (13:4). He had revealed Himself in covenant mercy and providential bounty—

> It was I who knew you in the wilderness,
> in the land of drought . . .

and the IVF *New Bible Commentary* points out that "a slight change of the Hebrew consonants gives a more plausible rendering (supported by LXX): 'I shepherded thee.' This is in better agreement with the context."

But—that word which so often mars the record of Israel's response to divine grace—

> . . . when they had fed to the full
> they were filled, and their heart was lifted up;
> therefore they forgot me (13:6).

And this story has been repeated in myriad lives, in all the intervening years. How many, in desperate need, have called upon God, and He has heard their cry and delivered them; but soon they forgot both Him and His mercy. Dr Martyn Lloyd-Jones, in telling why he abandoned a brilliant career in medicine to become a preacher, has described how burdened in spirit he was to witness men and women softened toward God in illness, and then, when restored to health, forget Him. It seemed to the young physician that he was, in assisting them medically, helping them to turn their backs upon God. Man is surely the most ungrateful of all God's creatures; and those He blesses most seem often to be the least thankful.

Therefore—again a word which recurs repeatedly in the Biblical narrative, providing a key to its exposition—"I will be to them as a lion . . . I will meet them as a bear robbed of her cubs" (13:7–8). It is noteworthy that David, the hero-king who made the nation great, had in his shepherd days slain a lion and a bear, which would have marauded his flock; now God uses these—together with the sinister leopard—as emblematic of His impending act of devastation. The One who, as the Shepherd of Israel, had so often protected them from their fearsome enemies, would be their destroyer; and He would use those enemies as His instrument. The doom so long foretold, was now upon them.

A bitter heart-cry was wrung from Hosea as, for the last time, he made the solemn pronouncement—"O Israel, thou hast destroyed thyself!" (13:9, *AV*), and indeed they had; but the more terrible note in the exclamation is conveyed by the *RSV*,

> I will destroy you, O Israel;
> Who can help you?

When Jehovah rises up in judgment against an apostate people, who indeed can help them! Israel, rejecting God as their King, had chosen kings of their own making. But what help had they been? What calamity they had led them into! Kings and people alike had come to the bar of judgment. No-one could save them.

> The iniquity of Ephraim is bound up,
> his sin is kept in store (13:12).

Stored up for the day of judgment! And that day had come.

15

Foregleams of Radiant Dawn

To discern a silver lining to the blackest thunder-cloud; to see foregleams of radiant dawn at the darkest hour of night, is prophetic vision indeed! Hosea's message to his people was, for the most part, stern and sombre; and he delivered it with steadfast persistence despite the fact that it was practically unheeded. Amid its stark warnings and ardent entreaty, however, there had occasionally sounded a more hopeful note of national rebirth; of regathering after the dispersal which would come upon Israel as the penalty of apostasy. As Hosea drew toward the close of his appointed ministry, this happier prospect increasingly possessed his soul, until finally this "blessed hope" suffused his whole message. His eyes were turned from his present distressful circumstances to that glorious daybreak of which he had already caught a distant glimmering. His last oracle to Israel (13 : 14—14 : 9) is one of glorious anticipation, blended with a final appeal that they would turn to the Lord, even at this late hour, in penitence and faith.

Consistently with his entire ministry, Hosea's vision of the future did not quench his concern for the people to whom he spoke the "word of the Lord." There is in his final utterance a remarkable interplay of judgment and mercy; of present circumstances and future prospect. Israel's sin would reap its reward; but despite their scattering in judgment God would achieve His purposes and fulfil His promises concerning His chosen people. God must ultimately triumph over all the machinations of the triumvirate of evil—the world, the flesh and the devil. Through all the tortured course of human history, He is accomplishing His end "unthwarted of all ill."

In the majestic onward march of God to the absolute realisation of His will and high calling for His people—Israel according to the flesh; and the church, according to the election of grace—He will never condone nor wink at sin. Inflexible judgment upon sin is an inviolable law of His governance in human affairs; and Calvary is the supreme expression of it. *There* judgment and mercy met together; *there* the Judge bore the penalty and secured the sinner's salvation. No other place of pardon can ever be found or provided; there can be no other mitigation of sin's consequences. The wages of sin is death. Many people—alas, many preachers—soft-pedal that fact today: but all Scripture testifies to it.

In virtue of that redemption wrought upon Calvary, however, all Scripture also links the proclamation of mercy with that of judgment—for the OT anticipated that "one offering for sin for ever" made by the "lamb slain from the foundation of the world." So in Hosea's passionate preaching to Israel, mercy keeps breaking in; the prophet repeatedly appeals to the people to repent and return to the Lord. This urgent entreaty runs through this closing section, even in the midst of glowing prediction regarding the future.

The prophet sounded forth the most awesome note of his message to Israel when he declared that "the sin of Ephraim is bound up; his sin is kept in store"—parcelled-up and ready for the blighting stroke of judgment (13:12). The hour of destiny had arrived: "the pangs of childbirth come for him"—but Israel did not read aright the signs of the times: "he is an unwise son; for now he does not present himself at the mouth of the womb" (13:13). Using the vivid imagery of childbirth, Hosea says that this might have been the time of new beginning, of spiritual re-birth, had the nation repented and sought the Lord: but in her folly Israel dallied—and died! Instead of presaging the joy of newness of life, therefore, the travail of Israel would herald her doom.

At that very point, the nadir of his prophecies, Hosea breaks forth into one of the most exultant of his predictions: "I will ransom them from the power of the grave; I will redeem them from death: O death, I will be thy plagues; O grave, I will be thy destruction . . ." (13:14). He is transported, as it were, right out of his own day and generation into the great and glorious "day of the Lord" when Israel shall greet her Messiah and the church her Saviour and Bridegroom. Sin, and its ultimate consequence, shall be swallowed up in victory! Maybe the pain of his pronouncement to his fellow-countrymen was more than Hosea could bear, and God gave him this glimpse of triumph yet to be, to relieve his own distress of spirit, and give him faith and courage to endure in his ministry to the end. Undoubtedly also there was a thrilling word of reassurance to the faithful remnant in Israel; and a testimony to all that God was not defeated, even by His people's sin, but would in the end fully realise His covenant pledges and purposes.

(While thus stating our own conviction concerning the interpretation of this verse, it must be acknowledged that scholars hold differing views as to its precise meaning. The Hebrew text is obscure; and quite a contrary implication—with which many students and commentators disagree—is conveyed by the *RSV*:

> Shall I ransom them from the power of Sheol?
>   Shall I redeem them from Death?
> O Death, where are your plagues?
>   O Sheol, where is your destruction?
>   Compassion is hid from my eyes.

This admittedly accords with the preceding verse. Thus read, it affirms that Israel's judgment will come upon them not only immediately, through Assyria, but also irredeemably. All the terrors of death and the grave would engulf them. The nation would be entirely extinguished. This rendering, however, deprives Hosea of one of his most exalted prophetic insights—which anticipated the apostle Paul's triumphant declaration regarding the final conquest of death, in 1 Corinthians 15 : 55–56. It is quite consistent with the whole character of this concluding oracle, that Hosea should alternate between contemporary circumstances and those of the final "day of the Lord".)

With swift return in thought from future prospect to present conditions, the prophet declares, "though he (Ephraim) be fruitful among his brethren, an east wind shall come, the wind of the Lord shall come up from the wilderness . . . and shall strip his treasury of every pleasant thing" (13: 15). There is here a play upon words, for the name "Ephraim" means "fruitful," and the tribe had certainly flourished more than others—and had complacently regarded their prosperity as proof of God's good pleasure. God would never chastise a people He favoured so manifestly! But Israel had not brought forth fruit unto God; therefore that prosperity should be taken from them. "Samaria shall bear her guilt . . ." and the prophet goes on to describe in terrifying terms the horrors about to be brought upon her by Assyria (13 : 16). Let it be clearly stated that these frightful tortures were not God's doing, nor did He sanction them. They were Assyria's way of waging war—and God would allow the invaders to conquer Israel because of their sin. His protecting mercy would be withdrawn, and Assyria would, in effect, become the rod of His chastisement upon the harlot nation. But God did not ordain nor condone their atrocities: Hosea is merely stating the stark facts concerning Assyrian conquest, without comment and certainly without commendation.

Even now it was not too late for a change of heart; and so in one last anguished entreaty Hosea cries, "O Israel, return unto the Lord thy God; for thou hast fallen by thine iniquity" (14:1). To spell out his appeal to them, he proceeds "Take with you words, and turn to the Lord: say unto Him, Take away all iniquity and receive us graciously: so will we render the calves of our lips" (14:2). This *AV* rendering robs the verse of its profoundest significance, however, for "calves" is a mis-translation: the *RSV* correctly translates the phrase, "we will render the *fruit* of our lips." Here Ephraim, ideally, is declaring that she will fulfil God's purpose declared in her very name, "Fruitful." This thought of true devotion being expressed by the lips is re-echoed by the writer to the Hebrews: "By Him (our Lord Jesus Christ) let us offer the sacrifice of praise to God continually, that is, the fruit of our lips giving thanks to His name" (Heb. 13:15).

Hosea then puts into the mouth of Israel—still ideally—a threefold confession, corresponding to their principal transgressions: "Asshur shall not save us; we will not ride upon horses; neither shall we say any more to the work of our hands, Ye are our gods . . ." (14:3). Here is disavowal of the covenant with the Assyrians (12:1) which in their folly they thought would save them from the predatory intentions of that greedy great power; here also is rejection of reliance upon Egypt and its method of making war on horseback; and finally, repudiation of idolatry. If indeed Israel had uttered this prayer, how different its story would have been!

Inspired by these thoughts, Hosea goes on to tell what Jehovah's response would be if Ephraim should thus call upon Him; and although, alas, they made no such immediate petition, yet the words of lustrous promise did not fall to the ground, but shall find fulfilment in that still future day of Israel's rebirth—"I will heal their backsliding, I will love them freely: for mine anger is turned away from him" (14:4). Could ever pledge be more forgiving and tender; love more longsuffering and compassionate than this of the divine Husband toward His unfaithful Gomer?

It seems as if Hosea were caught up in this apocalyptic vision, as the Lord goes on to assure His people, "I will be as the dew unto Israel..." (14 : 5). As the dew! But what a different significance this simile has when God uses it regarding the beneficent effect of His grace upon a truly repentant people, from His likening of their shallow profession of repentance to the early dew! Whereas their superficial confession was dispersed by the first rays of the rising sun, *His* lovingkindness would be inestimably reviving. As a result of it, "He (Ephraim) shall grow as the lily . . .": purity shall issue from the corruption of their former ways; "and cast forth his roots as Lebanon. His branches shall spread, and his beauty shall be as the olive tree, and his smell as Lebanon. They that dwell under his shadow shall return: they shall revive as the corn, and grow as the vine: the scent thereof shall be as the wine of Lebanon" (14:5–7).

Like a chime of bells, the threefold reference to Lebanon makes a pleasant harmony. "His roots as Lebanon" typifies strength and stability: for the way in which the famous cedars of Lebanon defied and withstood storm and tempest and scorching sun was proverbial (Psa. 92:12–14; Song of Solomon 5:15; Isa. 35:2). "His smell ('fragrance,' *RSV*) as Lebanon"—concerning which Fausset's *Cyclopaedia* says, "Odorous flowers and aromatic shrubs and vines still yield 'the smell of Lebanon' wafted by the mountain breeze," while the Song of Songs 4:11 says of the bridegroom, "the smell of thy garments is like the smell of Lebanon." And "the wine of Lebanon" was manifestly equally renowned: and wine in Scripture typifies rejoicing. Here is steadfastness, fragrance and fruitfulness —all that Ephraim lacked will be imparted to her, in that great day of the Lord!

With prophetic daring—and disregard of literary rules regarding mixed metaphors!—Hosea, having likened redeemed Israel to the cedars of Lebanon, transfers the simile to God himself, and speaks of Jehovah as the tree under whose spreading branches they shall find shelter and security (14:7). Their early promise shall at long last find full realisation: they shall "flourish as a garden" and "blossom as the vine." Israel, having learned her lesson through chastisement, will ask, rhetorically—signifying her complete renunciation of her former evil ways: "What have I to do any more with idols . . ." and the Lord will assure her, "From me is thy fruit found" (14:8), a final confirmation of Ephraim's discovery of the secret of her name. Their hearts' deepest desires shall be fully satisfied in Him, as His heart's deepest desires shall be fully satisfied in them.

Closely identified with his message as he has been throughout his ministry, and closely identified also with the people to whom he delivered it, Hosea in his very last word stands apart and exclaims—

Whoever is wise, let him understand these things;
  Whoever is discerning, let him know them;
for the ways of the Lord are right
  and the upright walk in them,
  but transgressors stumble in them.

The prophet has spoken faithfully all the "word of the Lord" committed to him. As always, it is a word of life to those who heed, and of death to those who disregard it. In affirmation of the divine sovereignty, Hosea declares that God is working His purposes out, and ultimately will fulfil all His promises and achieve all His ends. Yet in the impact of His word upon individual hearts and lives, He never violates the integrity of human freewill. It is the responsibility of every hearer to heed, to trust and obey; to walk with the Lord in the light of His word. In his very last sentence Hosea declares, in effect, that every son of man holds his soul's eternal destiny in his own hands.